W9-CPG-709

Pacific
LUMBER SHIPS

PACIFIC LUMBER

SHIPS

by
Gordon Newell
and
Joe Williamson

Bonanza Books • New York

LIBRARY OF CONGRESS CARD NUMBER 60-14426
PRINTED IN THE UNITED STATES OF AMERICA

This edition published by Bonanza Books,
a division of Crown Publishers, Inc.,
by arrangement with Superior Publishing Company
(A)

FOREWORD

PROBABLY the writing of this book was inevitable since the summer day in 1926 when I looked up from my youthful beachcombing on the shore of Budd Inlet on southern Puget Sound, amazed to see a pair of tall masts with long cargo booms gliding along behind behind a screen of salal and young madrona trees that sheltered the little cove of Gull Harbor from the main inlet.

In due time a stubby wooden bow appeared, a raised fo'csle, a stretch of open deck and, perched well aft, a neat white deckhouse, pilothouse, lifeboats and a smartly raked black funnel emitting clouds of heady oil smoke.

It was the steam schooner *Wapama,* headed for Olympia and a load of fir lumber. Olympia's harbor had just been dredged to accommodate seagoing ships that year and only one, the *Milan Maru* of the Japanese "K" Line, had called there before the *Wapama.* Sailing the narrow inlet she looked as big as the *Mauretania* and, to me, as exciting as Drake's *Golden Hind.*

The arrival of the *Wapama* marked the beginning of a love affair with the wooden steam schooners that lasted as long as they did and longer. Often accompanied by a boyhood friend, whose father was the local chief of police, I would visit the Olympia port dock to give unofficial welcome to every newly docked steam schooner—the *Jane Nettleton, Viking, John C. Kirkpatrick, Hartwood, Claremont* and a score of others.

There were big steel ships loading lumber at Olympia, too, but we gave our hearts to the brave little wooden steam schooners, whose days afloat were already numbered. Probably because the words written by Archie Binns in his book *Sea in the Forest* are among the eternal verities: *"A steel vessel leaves cold hearts that are warmed by the sight of a wooden one. Wooden steamers are warm and alive, and they never rot because they actually breathe."*

The crews of the steam schooners were remarkably tolerant of the small boys who had such obvious admiration for their little wooden ships. We drank strong coffee in galleys and spent bug-eyed hours in spotless engine rooms. The steam schooner men must have been possessed of deep patience, for I cannot recall that Bob and I were ever frog-marched ashore, except by a motorcycle policeman whom his father would dispatch to round us up when we overstayed the dinner hour too long. Then we would go bouncing off toward home, Bob astride the cycle behind the long-suffering policeman and I in the sidecar . . . and both of us with heads turned backward like those of barn owls for a last look at the beautiful steam schooner loading golden lumber in the sunset.

It is my hope that this book may have captured a bit of the tang of that vanished era when wooden ships with wooden cargos made their own brand of salty history offshore and in the sawmill ports of the Pacific Coast.

Gordon Newell, Seattle, Washington, September, 1960

FOREST OF MASTS AT PORT BLAKELY in the glory days of the Puget Sound mill ports, circa 1910; schooner *Blakely* in the foreground.

TAUT LINES AND FULL CANVAS carried Pacific Coast timber to world ports from Acapulco to Zanzibar.

A NIMBLE FOUR-MASTER was the *C. S. Holmes,* setting speed records on the Puget Sound to Fiji Islands run and from Grays Harbor to Guaymas. She's pictured on the opposite page at the start of a 1904 voyage from Port Blakely to Suva, which she completed in 38 days. She remained in service until World War II, long after other windjammers, like those above, were dismantled or laid up in harbor backwaters.

WHITE WATER TUGBOAT *Triumph* drags a three-masted lumber drougher across the Coquille River bar toward a safe mooring at the Coquille Mill Company dock. The *Triumph,* built at Parkersburg, Oregon in 1889, is still in service at Seattle.

Sometimes the sailing ships found a lee shore and no helpful tugboat. It happened to the brig *Courtney Ford,* lower left.

TYPICAL WOODEN STEAM SCHOONERS were the jaunty little 550-ton *Tiverton,* above, built at Hoquiam in 1906, and the larger 974-ton *Trinidad,* launched at Fairhaven in 1918. Both met violent ends, the *Tiverton* on Humboldt bar in 1933, the *Trinidad* on Willapa bar four years later.

WILLIAMS BOAT HOUSE
FERRY LANDING.

STEAM ENGINES AND CARGO BOOMS, above, have lost out to motor-cranes and barges towed by diesel tugs in present-day water transportation of lumber. Seagoing barges like the one at the right now carry many timber cargos between West Coast ports.

Barkentine *Amazon* in drydock.

ATERFRONT

PUGET SOUND SHIPPING

Reported by the Merchant's Exchange, Seattle

Handy Reference Table for Puget Sound—Corrected Semi-Weekly

NAME. FLAG AND RIG.	ARRIVED.	TN.	MASTER.	LOADING PORT	CARGO.	DESTINATION
Abner Coburn, Am sh	Apr. 22	1879	Burges	Winslow	Lumber	Nitrate Ports
Alex. T. Brown, Jc	Apr. 11	654	McKay	Tacoma	Lumber	San Pedro
Aloha, Am sc	Apr.	814	Dabel	Port Gamble	Lumber	San Francisco
Alpena, Am sc	Apr. 29	833	Lorenz	Puget Sound	Lumber	San Diego
Annie E. Smale, Am sc	Apr. 10	809	Colstrup	Everett	Lumber	San Pedro
Archer, bkt	Mar. 29	845	Nelson	Roche Harbor	Lime	San Francisco
Argo, Nor bk	Mar. 5	1533	Hendrickson	Port Blakeley	Lumber	West Coast
Arthur Fitger, Ger sh	Mar. 18	1696	Hopken	Port Blakeley	Lumber	Valparaiso
Balmoral, Br sh	April 18	2449	Roop	Port Blakeley	Lumber	Callao
Belen, Fr bk	Mar. 30	1731	Boudrot	Tacoma	Ballast	Australia
Blakeley, Am sc	Apr. 12	631	Chipperfield	Port Blakeley	Lumber	Redondo
Barnside, str	Feb. 13	1403	Laffin	Seattle		For orders
Californian, Am str	Apr. 29	3716	Sweetser	Seattle-Tacoma	General	Honolulu
Cloch, Br. bk	Apr. 10	1346	Lynn	Ludlow		West Coast
Crillon, Fr sh	Apr. 19	1734	Prado	Seattle-Tacoma	Wheat	United Kingdom
Dashing Wave, Am bge		941	Spinney	Repairing	Quartermaster	Harbor
Deanmount, Br sh	Apr. 13	1791	Mellin	Vancouver	Lumber	Iquique
Drumcliffe, Br str	Mar. 30	2599	Spurring	Bellingham	Lumber	Port Pirie
Durbridge, Br sh	Mar. 29	2120	Inglis	Tacoma	Lumber	Iquique
Earl of Dunmore, Br sh	Feb. 21	2205	Meneke	Vancouver	Lumber	Callao
Eldorado, sc	Apr. 1	790	Huhs	Everett	Poles	Redondo
Elsa, Nor. str	Apr. 12	2304	Morsoe	Tacoma	Lumber	Sydney
Empress of China, Br str	Apr. 28	3003	Archibald	Vancouver	General	Orient
Everett G. Griggs, Br bkt.	Jan. 31	2361	Delano	Chemainus	Lumber	Valparaiso
Eugenie Fautrel, Fr bk	Mar. 27	1705	Lehue	Seattle	Cement	Discharging
Fennia, Rus bk	Apr. 12	2154	Soderham	Mukilteo	Lumber	Iquique
Forteviot, Br bk	Jan. 30	2962	Finlay	Bellingham	Lumber	Adelaide
Gen. Fairchild, Am bk	Mar. 14	1307	Swain	Tacoma	Lumber	San Pedro
George C. Perkins, Am bk	Apr. 12	369	Gullickson	Tacoma	Lumber	Honolulu
Geo. E. Billings, Jc	Apr. 10	1103	Birkholm	Bellingham	Lumber	San Francisco
Georgia, Br str	Apr. 12	2022	Graalfs	Victoria		For orders
Georgia, Br str	Apr. 25	1778	Henderson	Vancouver	General	Mexico
Gladys, Br bk	Apr. 1	1345	Perrian	Tacoma	Coal	Guatemala
Haldis, Nor str	Feb. 9	1065	Jensen	Vancouver	General	Alaska
Harbart, Br str	Apr. 24	2149	Bowling	Nanaimo	Coal	San Francisco
Hesper, Bk	Apr. 9	603	Svendsen	Blakely	Lumber	San Francisco
Hornet, Am str	Apr. 24	402		Seattle-Tacoma	Lumber	San Francisco
Inveramsay, Br bk	Apr. 14	1321	Tobin	Tacoma	Lumber	Delagoa Bay
Ivy, Am sh	Apr. 5	1118	Stetson	Victoria		Repairing
Jas. Johnson, Am bkt	Apr. 29	997	Bennecke	Mukilteo	Lumber	San Pedro
Jean, Fr bk	Feb. 1	1706	Le Gal	Tacoma	Wheat	United Kingdom
John C. Potter, Am barge				Seward	Loading coke	At Electric Bunkers
Kaihlani, bk	Apr. 6	1436	Colly	Ludlow	Lumber	San Francisco
Klikitat, Am bkt	Apr. 25	432	Cutler	Port Gamble	Lumber	Honolulu
Kona, Am sc	Apr. 29	642	Sjostrom	Port Blakeley	Lumber	San Diego
La Richejaquelin, Fr bk	Mar. 14	1953	Durand	Tacoma	Wheat	U. K., H., A. or D.
Leelanaw, Am str	Mar. 23	1378	Meyer	Seattle	Coal	California
Luzon, Am sc	Apr. 29	512	Nelson	Everett	Lumber	San Diego
Marguerite Dollfus, Fr b	Jan. 5	1604	Ticheaux	Tacoma	Wheat	United Kingdom
Marion Josiah, Br sh	Dec. 5	2257	Grant	Tacoma	Wheat	United Kingdom
Mashona, Nor sh	Apr. 27	2303	Broch	Vancouver	Lumber	Valparaiso
Matterhorn, Br sh	Mar. 26	1754	Morell	Seattle	Cement	Discharging
Maweema, Am sc	Apr. 22	392	Smith	Tacoma	Lumber	San Diego
Melanope, Br bk	Apr. 1	1564	Wills	Nanaimo		
Mildred, sc	Apr. 11	411		Bellingham	Lumber	San Pedro
Missouri, Am str	Apr. 26	5077	Tilton	Seattle-Tacoma	General	Honolulu
Muskoka, Br bk	Mar. 30	2259	McDonald	Tacoma	Lumber	West Coast
Najade, Ger sh	Mar. 19	1677	Van Der Loo	Port Gamble	Lumber	West Coast
Needles, Br str	Apr. 12	2995	Turner	Tacoma	Lumber	Australia
Newsboy, Am bkt	Apr. 29	509	Olsen	Tacoma	Lumber	San Pedro
Oanfa, Br str	Apr. 24	5676	Riley	Tacoma	General	Yokohama
Oceania Vance, sc	April 19	381		Tacoma	Lumber	San Francisco
Okanogan, Am sc	Apr. 7	606	Mather	Port Gamble	Lumber	San Francisco
Oscar II., Nor str	Apr. 25	1999	Wilhelmsen	Port Blakeley	Lumber	Shanghai
O. J. Olsen, Am sc	Apr. 29	595	Kallenberg	Everett	Lumber	San Diego
Pleiades, str	Apr. 5	2932	Purrington	Seattle		For orders
Redondo, Am str	Apr. 21	462		Tacoma	Lumber	San Francisco
Regina Elena, It bk	Apr. 19	2148	Merella	Port Blakeley	Lumber	Delagoa Bay
Riverside, Br sh	Mar. 27	1590	Jenkins	Tacoma	Lumber	Valparaiso
Salem, Am sc	Apr. 22	698	Anderson	Olympia	Lumber	San Pedro
Saratoga, str	Apr. 10	1973	Moore	Seattle		Repairing
Sardhana, Br bk	Mar. 27	1119	Walker	Vancouver	Lumber	United Kingdom
Schwartzenbek, Ger sh	Mar. 4	1377		Fraser River	Lumber	Callao
Senator, Br sh	Feb. 12	1580	Kinney	Tacoma	Lumber	Valparaiso
Servia, Br bk	Apr. 16	1736	Nelson	Ladysmith		Karluk
Sheila, Br str	Mar. 27	2237	Ogilvie	Vancouver	General	Departure Bay
Snow & Burgess, Am sc	Apr. 29	1528	Sorenson	Port Gamble	Lumber	San Francisco
Tarpenbek, Ger bk	Mar. 20	1767	Bruhn	Chemainus	Lumber	West Coast
Tartar, Br str	April 19	2768	Davidson	Vancouver	General	Yokohama
Tellus, Nor str	Apr. 27	1612	Berg	Nanaimo	Coal	San Francisco
Tildra, Nor str	Apr. 24	2097	Christiansen	Comox	Coal	San Francisco
Tolosan, Ger str	Apr. 22	2089	Jebsen	Seattle-Tacoma	Flour	China
Tordenskjold, Nor str	Apr. 27	2296	Hansen	Nanaimo	Coal	San Francisco
Victoria, Am str	Nov. 7	2112		Seattle		Disengaged
Wellington, Br str	Apr. 6	1267	Cutler	Ladysmith	Coal	San Francisco
W. F. Babcock, Am sh	Feb. 13	1993	Stimson	Port Townsend	Lumber	Manila
Willesden, Br str	Apr. 5	3141	Raeburn	Hadlock	Lumber	West Coast
Woodford, Br str	Feb. 20	1360	Seddon	Vancouver	Lumber	Australia

LUMBER TRADE WAS AT ITS HEIGHT a half century ago, as indicated by this 1907 Puget Sound shipping record showing a total of 52 vessels loading timber cargos there on a single day.

Chapter 1
SHIPS OF SAIL

Square-rigged ship *St. Frances.*

SIX decades ago, in the early years of the twentieth century, the northwest corner of America was a sawdust frontier empire of tall mountains, tall trees and tall masts. Lumber was sailing the sea roads from Puget Sound to all the ports of the civilized world; sailing in the true sense of the word . . . under canvas. This was the last stronghold of the most beautiful of men's creations—the ships whose only power was the wind.

The Puget Sound shipping register for mid-April, 1902, was typical of that era. It listed as loading lumber at Port Blakely the British square-rigged ships *King George* and *Bann* and the bark *Kelverdale,* together with the American bark *Prussia,* brig *Tanner* and the schooners *Inca, Bainbridge, R. W. Bartlett, James A. Garfield, Honoiyu, H. D. Bendixson* and *John D. Tallant.*

At Tacoma mill docks lay the British ships *Laomene* and *Troop,* the American barkentines *Charles F. Crocker* and *Gardiner City,* and the schooners *Metha Nelson, Endeavor, Glendale, J. M. Weatherwax, Luzon, Marion, Salvator* and *Annie Larson.*

The great mill at Port Gamble was feeding timber to a fleet of windjammers that included the square-rigged *Scottish Hills* and the clipper bark *Tidal Wave* along with the barkentine *Skagit* and the schooners *Gamble, William Olsen, John G. North, Ida Schnauer, Maria E. Smith* and *Queen.*

The barkentines *Amazon* and *J. M. Griffiths* and the schooners *Roy Somers* and *C. S. Holmes* were at Port Hadlock and the schooners *Joseph Russ, Bangor* and *Ethel Zane* at Port Ludlow. At Seattle were the British ship *Arctic Stream* and the schooners *Columbia, Albert Meyer* and *Wempe Bros.*

Across the International Boundary at Vancouver and Chemainus were the German ship *Ostara* and bark *Pallas,* the Norwegian square-rigger *Prince Louis* and the American bark *Challenger* and schooner *Forester.*

The three-masted American bark *Vidette* was loading from barges in the stream at Olympia, head of navigation on Puget Sound and the Italian bark *Cavour* and the American schooner *Solano* at Everett, seventy miles down sound. Another sixty miles north, at the twin cities of Whatcom and Fairhaven, were the schooners *William Renton* and *Fearless* and the Japanese steamship *Shakano Maru.*

The *Shakano Maru,* loading rough timbers for Shanghai, was the only steam powered vessel among the 55 ships that were loading lumber on Puget Sound in the month of April, 1902.

The square-rigged ships and the big Cape Horn barks would carry their cargos to Cork, Fremantle, Iquiqui and Melbourne. To Cardiff, Taku Bar, Calcutta, Callao, Port Natal and Delagoa Bay. Some of the deep-sea schooners and barkentines were destined for Honolulu, Guaymas, Tahiti, Santa Rosalia and the Fijis, but most of the smaller ships were in the coastwise trade. Commanded by Captains Johnsen, Johnston, Jensen, Neilson, Nielsen, Anderson, Andersen, Liljqvist or Holmquist, they formed the "Scandinavian Navy" that carried northwest timber to the ports of San Francisco and San Pedro.

Probably the first sailing ships to make their landfall off the West Coast of the American continent were primitive Oriental junks, caught in the eastward drift of *Kura Shima,* the Japanese Current, and cast up at last on a strange and savage shore. Indian legends tell of yellow-skinned men thus cast ashore and sometimes adopted by the tribes, perhaps hundreds of years before the coming of the first white men's ships. History records that, between 1833 and 1875, sixty Chinese and Japanese craft were wrecked along the Pacific Coast from Baja California to the Aleutian Islands.

European ships first sailed these waters when, in 1519, the renegade Portuguese pilot Magellan led a Spanish exploration fleet through the straits which bear his name, leading the way for the creation of New Spain and the entry of stately Spanish galleons to the first Pacific trade routes with Europe and the Orient.

Spanish domination of the Pacific ended in 1578 with the arrival of the British sea rover (pirate, the Spanish called him) Francis Drake, who sailed his *Golden Hind* through the Straits of Magellan and went swashbuckling up the coast leaving a trail of looted ships and plundered ports in his wake. After sailing as far north, probably, as the present coast of Washington in a futile search for the fabled Straits of Anian, Drake reversed his course, eluded aroused Spanish warships and returned to England to trade his shipload of Spanish loot for a knighthood and an admiral's flag in the queen's navy.

In the years that followed the ships of Russia, England and Spain sailed the coastal waters of the Pacific, but the shores they skirted were, for the most part, grimly inhospitable. There was little desire on the part of shipmasters to venture too close to the spouting breakers and offshore reefs to determine what bays or straits or river mouths were hidden in the sea mists.

It was in 1792 that Captain George Vancouver, commanding His Majesty's Sloop-of-War *Discovery,* hove-to off what is now the Washington coast to pass the time of day with the Yankee merchant skipper Robert Gray of the ship *Columbia.*

From this chance meeting the *Discovery,* with the armed tender *Chatham,* sailed north to discover and chart the waters of Puget Sound. The *Columbia* sailed south to discover and chart the waters of Grays Harbor and the legendary River of the West, which was henceforth to bear the name of Gray's ship, the *Columbia.* For countless centuries the far northwest coast of America had remained a virtually unknown land. In the space of a few weeks Vancouver and Gray placed the area in the well mapped atlas of discovery. One thing these newly discovered waterways had in common; they were surrounded by brooding forests of colossal height. The raw material for the sawdust empire of the Pacific Northwest had been waiting centuries for the harvest.

It was to be another half century, however, before the potential value of these western forests began to be realized. True, Russian colonists from Siberia hunting sea otter in southern waters, put ashore in the redwood country of northern California in 1811 to establish a trading post and water-powered sawmill, but when Captain Smith of the bark *George Henry* reached the Pacific Coast in 1840 he was amazed to find that lumber for California was shipped in from the Sandwich Islands.

Being a canny New Englander with an eye for profit, Captain Smith picked up the essential parts for a sawmill on his next voyage east. The mill was erected in the redwood forest near Bodega and by 1843 the *George Henry* had established a pattern and earned herself a place in history. She was carrying lumber coastwise to San Francisco. Until then the ships of the West Coast fleet had been intent on the fabulous profits of the fur trade or the liquid gold of the northern whaling grounds.

By 1847 the brigs *Janet* and *Henry* were carrying small shipments of lumber, along with such general cargo as "flour, salmon, beef, potatoes, butter, cheese, cranberries, turnips, cabbages, onions and nine passengers" between the Columbia River and San Francisco.

It was two years later, in September of 1849, that a modest little brig of 140 tons, the *Oriental,* set sail from Talbot wharf in East Machias, Maine. Ostensibly her cargo consisted of 600,000 feet of Maine lumber destined for gold rush San Francisco, two house frames, an assortment of joists and timber and a small consignment of shingles. It wasn't listed on her manifest, but the *Oriental* was also carrying the seeds of an industrial empire to the far northwest coast of America.

STOUT LUMBER SCHOONER *Susie M. Plummer,* opposite page, went missing on a 1909 voyage from Everett for San Pedro. Her wreckage was found on Vancouver Island the following year, but no trace of her 12-man crew was ever found.

SQUARED TIMBERS FROM THE NORTHWEST FORESTS provide a hefty deckload for the big World War I-built wooden schooner *General Pershing.* Loading was taking place from dockside and barges by ship's tackle when this early post-war photograph was taken in Seattle harbor.

Although she was no clipper, the *Oriental* made a creditable passage around Cape Horn as might be expected of a veteran Maine seaman like her master, Captain William Talbot. Upon his arrival in San Francisco, Captain Talbot found that his brother Fred, who had sailed to California six months before, had conveniently formed a partnership with Andrew Pope. They were in the retail lumber business. Their stock in trade was being supplied by Captain Lafayette Balch, who was bringing down cargos of lumber from his new town of Steilacoom on Puget Sound, but they were sure they could dispose of the *Oriental's* cargo in San Francisco and up the river at Sacramento.

As San Francisco boomed, burned periodically and was rebuilt to boom and burn again, it became apparent to the Talbot brothers and Pope that vast profits awaited such enterprising business men as might find a means of delivering large quantities of lumber to San Francisco at reasonable prices. The obvious answer was to build a big sawmill somewhere in the forests to the north and make the *Oriental* the nucleus of a fleet of coastwise lumber carriers.

Humboldt Bay had been found and settled in 1848 and it was ringed with great redwood forests. A single tree would yield twice as much lumber as could be stowed aboard the little coastal brigs of that era and Humboldt Bay was close to the San Francisco market. But Pope and Talbot were determined to ship lumber, not just cut and mill it. The bay offered safe anchorage once a ship was inside, but its bar could be dangerous; sometimes deadly.

In 1851 Andrew Pope and William Talbot formed

a partnership with Captain J. P. Keller for the purpose of building and operating "a Steam Saw Mill for manufacturing lumber in Oregon Territory in the vicinity of Puget Sound." They had decided, all factors considered, that the "Oregon pine" country of Puget Sound offered the best future to a budding lumber dynasty.

The redwood forests were not long neglected, however. By 1852 San Francisco promoter Harry Meiggs had a steam sawmill puffing away at Mendocino City and another was being built at Crescent City. By 1860 some 300 mills were gnawing away at the redwoods. By the mid-1880's there were more than four hundred operating in the Humboldt forest region alone.

Pope and Talbot had, in the meantime, returned home to Maine, added cousin Charles Foster to the partnership, loaded his fine new schooner *L. P. Foster* with mill machinery and skilled workers and conveyed their families back to San Francisco. From there Captain Talbot set out in the fifty-ton schooner *Julius Pringle* to search out a suitable mill site on Puget Sound. He found what he wanted on the shores of Discovery Bay, seventy miles up sound from the open Pacific. The deep, sheltered anchorage was ringed with immense trees whose trunks rose a hundred feet or more before they branched. Uncounted millions of feet of good clear lumber awaited the arrival of the *L. P. Foster* and her cargo of mill machinery, but Talbot decided that, good as this was, there might be better beyond.

Cruising slowly inland through the broad reaches of the Strait of Juan de Fuca, Admiralty Inlet and Puget Sound, the party was divided between a ship's boat commanded by Captain Talbot and an Indian canoe piloted by Cyrus Walker, who was to be resident manager of the new mill when it was built. They soon found that other enterprising pioneers were embarked on ventures similar to theirs. W. P. Sayward, another Maine man, was busily erecting a mill at a forested cove on Admiralty Inlet, a place which was to be called Port Ludlow.

Further inland, on the shore of broad Elliott Bay, they sighted the distant flutter of steam below a smudge of wood smoke. This was the new village of Seattle with its steam sawmill, erected by Henry Yesler in March of that year of "firsts," 1853. Washington had become an independent territory that year, too, separated from Oregon and with a governor of its own, Isaac I. Stevens, organizing his territorial capital at Olympia. The first American steamboat had arrived to ply between Seattle and Olympia and the settlers on Elliott Bay were celebrating other solid accomplishments . . . the town's

Above, top to bottom: *Muriel,* 536-ton schooner, was built at Alameda in 1895. *Wm. G. Irwin,* 350-ton brig, ended her days in the Roche Harbor lime trade. *Robt. E. Lewers,* four-master of 733 tons, was Hall-built at Port Blakely in 1889. *Lahaina,* 1067-ton barkentine, was launched at Oakland in 1901.

DECKLOAD OF PILING higher than foc'sle and quarterdeck topped off and well lashed down, the schooner *Andy Mahoney* will soon be off on another coastwise voyage between Grays Harbor and San Francisco. The *Mahoney* was built at Aberdeen in 1902.

first marriage and the opening of the first post office and hotel.

The explorers moved on, touching at Appletree Cove, where J. J. Felt had another small mill ready to start sawing, at a small harbor which later became Port Madison and at other likely spots along the solidly forested shores of Puget Sound. Cyrus Walker circled Vashon Island in his Indian canoe.

They finally decided on a location just inside Hood Canal where a small peninsula gave shelter to a deep-water bay and a level sand spit provided an ideal building site for the proposed mill. The Indians called this spot *Teekalit,* but it was destined to become the mill town of Port Gamble.

Leaving Cyrus Walker to direct the construction crew in the erection of bunkhouses, cookshack and mill foundations, Captain Talbot took time to carry a profitable cargo of milled lumber from Henry Yesler's wharf to San Francisco before he took the *Pringle* out to meet the *Foster* inbound and "loaded to the decks to the water with engine, boilers, mill machinery, merchandise for the store and supplies."

By mid-September the Port Gamble mill was hard at work, turning out 2000 feet of lumber a day, adding this modest output to that of the other steam sawmills at Seattle, Port Ludlow and Appletree Cove. The following year a big sash saw was installed to replace the original little "muley" and a marvelous device called a "live gang" was added. Its multiple blades could saw an entire log into planks with one operation and the mill's output skyrocketed to almost fifteen thousand feet a day.

Industrial revolution had come to the last frontier. Sailing ships from San Francisco which, a few years earlier had been limited to sparse coastwise cargo pickings of Willamette River garden produce, Shoalwater Bay oysters and occasional small consignments of hand-hewn timbers and piling on Puget Sound, found full cargos of lumber awaiting them at the Northwest mills. Settlers trying to grub a living from forest-choked land claims found their timber had suddenly become an asset instead of a liability, and there was work to be had at the mills to provide a cash income.

By 1857 Marshal Blinn's mill at Seabeck, also on Hood Canal, was gnawing away at the primeval forest and the shipping business was so good that Pope and Talbot had combined forces with George Meigs, who was operating a new mill at Port Madison, to bring up a tugboat, the *Resolute,* from San Francisco. Blinn soon had a shipyard in operation at Seabeck and the first hull to go down the ways was that of a stubby side-wheel tug, the *Colfax*. Within a few years a fleet of sturdy seagoing work horses were straining away at long booms of logs on Puget Sound or bucking the Pacific swells off Cape Flattery waiting to tow the lumber ships to the mill docks.

The ship building business was a natural result of the growing Pacific Northwest lumber industry, for both the mill companies and independent ship operators were intent on building up fleets to take advantage of the boom in coastwise trade. By 1861 the Pope and Talbot enterprise had become the Puget Mill Company, operating its own fleet of ten sailing vessels, the *Francisco, Constitution, Hyack, Jenny Ford, Kutusoff, Leonore, Oak Hill, Torrent, Vernon* and *Victor*. But all ten ships had a combined carrying capacity of only three and a half million feet of lumber, which is far less than can be carried by a single average sized freighter of today. It required a lot of small ships to haul the big cargos of lumber and the shipyards sprang up from San Francisco to Puget Sound. Hans Bendixsen went into the business in 1865 and turned out more than a hundred little wooden ships in the thirty years he plied his trade at Fairhaven on Humboldt Bay. Half a hundred yards were in the business before the era of the wooden lumber ship was ended, building schooners and barkentines and, finally, steam schooners. On Grays Harbor John Lindstrom at Aberdeen, G. H. Hitchings and Matthews at Hoquiam built wooden ships of sail and steam. Heukendorf and

Above, top to bottom: The 175-foot *Alert* was launched at Hoquiam in 1902, the four-masted, 600-ton *Robert Searles* at Port Blakely in 1888 for James Tuft of San Francisco. Dismasted and abandoned off Hawaii in 1913 with one crew member drowned, she was salvaged and converted to a barge. The 229-foot square-rigger *A. J. Fuller* was rammed and sunk by the Japanese steamer *Mexico Maru,* still lies under 250 feet of water in Seattle harbor. Schooner *Robert R. Hind* flew the Hind Rolph Shipping Company houseflag, carried many lumber cargos for Pope and Talbot, who owned a one-sixteenth interest in her.

A TUGBOAT WAS MIGHTY HANDY for an offshore or coastal windjammer of the lumber fleet. Many of the smaller harbors and river bars of the Pacific Coast can be hazardous to powered vessels and, before the tugboat era, sailing vessels sometimes took longer getting into Puget Sound after making their landfall off Cape Flattery than was consumed by the entire passage from the Hawaiian Islands.

The schooner *Vigilant,* commanded by Captain Matt Peasley of Peter B. Kyne's sea tales, is pictured above from the tug *Goliah.* Famed for her races between Cape Flattery and Hawaii with the *Commodore,* the *Vigilant* ended her days as the Canadian Transport Company's *City of Alberni,* was the last sailing vessel to carry lumber on the Pacific.

With topsails and topgallants being furled, the British bark *Battle Abbey,* below, is almost hidden by a Columbia River bar roller, but a stout hawser connects her with the bar tug from which the photograph was taken.

INBOUND IN BALLAST, the big windjammers which hauled lumber, coal and grain cargos from Puget Sound to ports across the Pacific or around Cape Horn, were particularly dependent on the services of tugboats. The two Puget Sound coal-burners, above, were working hard as they pulled the iron-hulled British bark *Ganges* toward her up-Sound loading port.

The Columbia River bar tug *Oneonta,* pictured below after dropping the line from a laden four-masted bark, served hundreds of sailing vessels from her station at Astoria. A steel steamer of 950 horsepower, the *Oneonta* was built at Portland in 1910, especially designed for her dangerous trade.

TANDEM TOWS saved time and money, but a tugboat skipper had to be alert to keep from getting his lines crossed. The *Azalea* and *Wawona* are pictured above sharing a tugboat on the Strait of Juan de Fuca, while the barks *Portland* and *Tidal Wave* and barkentine *Wm. Griffith,* right, prove that three is quite a crowd when attached to a single tug.

Top: The little three-masted lumber drougher *Maryann* gets an assist across the Humboldt Bar on a placid day in 1905, courtesy of the gallant bar tug *Ranger,* from whose stern the lower photograph, showing the schooner *Eric* crossing the bar, was taken.

Top: Steam tug *North King* towing wooden ship *Burgess* off British Columbia coast. Center: Tug *Tatoosh* picking up the schooner *Camano* off Cape Flattery. Below: Tug *Gleaner* towing schooner *Sadie* across the Umpqua River bar, lighthouse tender *Heather* following.

BUSY ESCORT TO THE LUMBER FLEET on Puget Sound was the old side-wheel towboat *Favorite,* pictured above at the Port Blakely Mill dock. Built at Utsalady, Washington in 1868 for the Grennan and Cranney Mill, the *Favorite* later towed logs and lumber ships for Pope and Talbot at Port Gamble and Port Ludlow, Meiggs and Gawley at Port Madison and the Port Blakely Mill Company. She lasted until 1920, when she was dismantled at Seattle, the era of side-wheel steamboats and wind-powered lumber ships having ended.

The three-masted schooner *Advance,* below, was outward bound across the Bandon bar when her photograph was taken back in 1906. Packing a mighty deckload and bucking a rainsquall, her crew probably appreciated the mill tug up ahead, which didn't get in the picture.

the Kruse & Banks yard at North Bend, Oregon, Matthew Turner at San Francisco, John Dickie at Alameda and Thomas H. Peterson on the redwood coast built their share of sturdy wooden ships, but the greatest of them all was the Hall Brothers yard, which operated at Port Ludlow from 1874 until 1880 and then, from 1881 until 1905, at Port Blakely. During these years the yard turned out 109

BRITISH COLUMBIA WORKHORSE was the big steam tug *Active,* left top, built at New Westminster in 1889 for the Hastings Lumber Company and used for ship and log towing.

Tug *Astoria,* next lower, was one of the early Oregon Coast bar tugs.

The *Haro* was another of the Hastings Lumber Company's Vancouver-based mill tugs.

The *Richard Holyoke,* lower left, was built by the Seabeck Mill Company in 1877, named for the mill's general manager. The *Holyoke* was having little trouble moving the three-master *Vega* when this 1910 photograph was taken.

A breaking bar meant hard and dangerous work for offshore tugboats like the *Oneonta,* pictured above as she bulldozed her way through smashing seas toward a sailing ship off the Columbia.

ships, almost all sailing vessels. The 110th, a steam schooner, was built at Winslow in 1905.

The skilled shipwrights of the little yards which turned out wooden coasters were craftsmen and rugged individualists and they did not survive the change from hewing axe and caulking hammer to welding torch and riveter. And something of their individuality and character seemed to be built into their ships to be passed on to the men who sailed

DECKLOAD . . .

Towering deckloads were a trademark of the lumber ships. Many of the small wooden schooners and steam schooners were designed to carry more of their cargo "out in the open" than in the holds. The *Andy Mahoney,* above, was heaped with mine props for Santa Rosalia, Mexico until there was barely room for her booms to swing. The *Albert Meyer,* left center, had rough lumber piled well above her deckhouse tops and the big four-poster *Columbia,* lower left, packed a full load of piling on this voyage from Bellingham to San Francisco.

Other typical deckloads of sailing ship days are pictured on the opposite page aboard the barkentine *Thos. P. Emegh,* top, four-masted schooners *Robert R. Hind* and *Fred J. Wood,* center.

them along the coast of northern California, Oregon and Washington.

The crews of the coastal lumber fleet worked without benefit of steam power to turn propellers and cargo winches as they skirted a shoreline which provided few havens for seamen in distress. Humboldt Bay and Crescent City provided the only real harbors on California's redwood coast and they

weren't easy to enter when things were kicking up off shore. The Columbia River bar, between Oregon and Washington, was an authentic ship's graveyard for windjammmers in trouble and the entrances to Willapa and Grays Harbor on the Washington Coast were not always hospitable either. The entrance to Puget Sound, at Cape Flattery, was twelve miles wide, but the winds there were particularly tricky and the outward set of the tide could combine with the northward drift of the ocean current to turn a shipmaster's hair white in short order.

As mill sites on the more sheltered waterways were spoken for, the lumber business spread to less likely locations. Redwood mills sprang up along the rocky Mendocino coastline and offered cargos to shipmasters daring or foolhardy enough to come and

SHIPS THAT MEET . . .

The deep-laden lumber schooners *Prosper* and *Fred E. Sander,* having dropped their tug off Cape Flattery, square away for the coastwise run to San Francisco.

get them. Cargo loading was a matter of clinging to anchors under a loading chute within spitting distance of spouting breakers and deadly reefs. These rocky indentations were known as dogholes, although few sensible dogs would be caught dead in one of them if there was any way to avoid it.

Such skin-of-the-teeth navigational and loading procedures were all in a day's work for the hard-bitten sea dogs of the lumber droughers, however, and it is no wonder that they were a tough and colorful breed. Transplanted Swedes, Norwegians and Danes seemed to gravitate naturally to the lumber ships, perhaps because the stormy seas and narrow, rock-girt harbors they were required to sail were somewhat like the fiord-pierced Scandinavian coast.

There was a total lack of spit and polish on the lumber schooners and their masters were generally known by such informal appellations as Flatfoot Hanson, Midnight Olsen and Pieface Johnson. Deep sea ship's officers might look down their noses at the rough-and-ready discipline and "by-guess-and-by-God" navigating techniques of the schoonermen, but they took their little ships in and out of places that would have given their offshore colleagues the screaming mimies. Jerry MacMullen tells of the schooner skipper who was explaining his methods of navigation to a sailor as follows:

"I takes me a lonnitude und from dat I works out a laddidude. If it don't come out vere I t'ink ve should be . . . vy de hell mit dat lonnitude und I takes me anudder vun!"

The skipper of a two-master plying between Oregon's Umpqua River and San Francisco was once

SHIPS THAT PASS . . .

Inward bound in ballast, the schooner *Wm. H. Smith,* in the foreground, passes the outward bound *Andy Mahoney* off the Grays Harbor bar.

visited by a local schoolteacher and her class. When queried by the teacher as to how he managed to find his way through fog, storm and rain from the Umpqua to the Golden Gate he scratched his head a bit and uttered this even more classic statement:

"Vy, I *been* dar!"

The folksy atmosphere of the coastwise schooners was heightened by the fact that their crews generally remained with them for more than one voyage. In the case of the bigger offshore ships, which spent more time obtaining cargos and loading them, the crews were usually paid off in Port Townsend, port of entry for Puget Sound, and the vessels were towed to the up-sound mill docks manned only by officers, bos'n, carpenter and sailmaker.

As a result, Port Townsend became a salty seaport in the epic tradition, with a bay full of tall-masted ships awaiting cargos or, outward bound, pausing long enough to ship new crews. The Port Townsend waterfront was lined with sailors' boarding houses, saloons and brothels. Crimping . . . the supplying of seamen to shipmasters at a price . . . was big business and when manpower was at a premium, knock-out drops and trap-doors in saloon floors were the tools of the crimp's trade.

The respectable citizens of Port Townsend, and many of the ship captains, lived on the bluff above the waterfront, where substantial Victorian houses graced neat, tree-lined streets. There were churches there, and schools and even a separate business district where sober people could do their marketing without being shocked by the goings-on down under the bluff.

But the crews came from Townsend-Under-the-

ROLLING DOWN TO HILO, the schooner *Commodore,* above, made a lovely picture at the close of the windship era as gulls escorted her past Cape Flattery at the beginning of a 1931 voyage to the Hawaiian Islands.

The six-masted barkentine *Everett G. Griggs,* opposite, was an unusual member of the Pacific lumber fleet. Launched at Belfast in 1883 as a conventional four-masted bark, the *Lord Wolseley,* she was dismasted off Cape Flattery in 1905. The wreck was purchased by a Seattle group including lumberman Everett G. Griggs and steamship operators Joshua Green and Charles Peabody, renamed and given her novel rig, the six-master ended her days as the *E. R. Sterling;* was broken up for scrap in England after another dismasting in 1928.

Bluff. It wasn't quiet there, and it wasn't respectable, not that narrow slice of the town at sea level between the sleeping fleet in the bay and the sleeping homes on the hill. It stayed open all night, did Townsend-Under-the-Bluff. Wide open.

The red lights shone bright in the night from the crib houses down by the docks. No cheese cloth draped over them here as it was up the Sound at Seattle, where the mayor was trying to make the Skid Road respectable, and not much draping on the blowsy women who leaned from the upstairs windows and called to the men on the street.

The men on the street were mostly sailors and loggers and blue-uniformed artillerymen from the seacoast forts. They had a wide choice of diversions, and none of them were healthy. Some were worse than others, of course. The red-lighted "hotels" of Water Street were havens of refuge compared to the squaw houses further down the beach by Point Hudson where one night with the renegade gamblers and poisonous liquor and half-breed slatterns could ruin a man for life.

But most dangerous of all were the waterfront saloons. There was a saloon for every 75 men, women, and children of Townsend's population at the turn of the century, and almost all of them were within a bottle-toss of salt water. Many of them were closer than that, their back rooms supported on piling driven into the bay bottom. For it was in the saloons that the crews were prepared for shipment to the windjammers waiting offshore, and those back rooms were convenient for the purpose.

The process was simple and routine, like any other well organized industry. Take the true and typical case of John Sutton, American citizen, aged 23, logger by trade:

Above, top to bottom: Barkentine *Gardiner City,* top, was later rerigged and renamed as the four-masted schooner *Kitsap,* next lower.

Four-master *Bainbridge,* riding high, was headed for Puget Sound mill dock and lumber cargo. *Commerce* was outward bound, fully loaded.

When the logging camp where John was working was shut down because it was in the path of one of the annual summer forest fires that consumed miles of virgin timber in the foothills of the Olympic Mountains, he drew his pay and headed for the nearest town; Port Townsend. By the time he had his money spent, he knew, the Autumn rains would have ended the forest fires for another year and the camp would open up again; or, if not, he could find another camp. Every one knew there was no limit to the virgin timber stands of the Northwest Coast.

Of course John Sutton went to Water Street. There was no welcome up on the Bluff for a young timber beast in stagged pants and cork boots with a bundle of dirty blankets on his shoulder. But there was ample welcome on Water Street. Water Street was geared to handle people just like John Sutton.

The red lights didn't attract young John much. Neither did the naked Siwash girls who peddled their bodies with bovine acquiescence at the squaw houses on the edge of town. A drink or two and maybe a sociable game of cards was more in his line.

He found both at the Blue Light Saloon, down on the Union Dock. The whiskey was honest, but the card dealer wasn't. It was Hudson's Bay whiskey, brought across the Straits at night and unloaded through the trap door over the bay. The Customs House on the hill had no record of the shipment, nor of most of the other shipments that ended up in the waterfront saloons. The card dealer had come across the Straits from Canada, too, a deserter from a British warship in for repairs at Esquimalt.

When John Sutton's last gold piece was in the pot on the green table, the English gambler gave the bartender a brief nod. "This one's on the house, friend," the bartender said as he refilled John's glass from a bottle that looked just like all the others . . . except for a minute tear in one corner of the label.

John Sutton never played that last hand. When the knockout drops began to wear off, 20 hours later, he was on the vomit-smeared foc'sl deck of a three-masted bark in the open Pacific, a hundred miles off Cape Flattery and outward bound for Australia. He didn't know that when he first began coming back to life. All he was sure of was that he was deathly, inhumanly sick; and somebody was kicking him hard in the belly—kicking and cursing him savagely and expertly.

He didn't know either, what had happened after he took his last drink at the Blue Light Saloon in Port Townsend. It had been a standard operation. When the young logger slumped forward, face down among the bright cards on the green gambling table, a smooth team play was begun. A hard faced character in a derby hat left a nearby table to help the bartender support the limp figure into the back room . . . the room with the bay under the floor.

The bartender rifled pockets expertly, while the derbied plug-ugly unlaced the high logger boots. They were good ones, hand-made and worth twenty dollars second hand. They missed nothing of value. When they were through, the bartender's assistant departed for his headquarters. He was a "runner" for the city's leading firm of flesh-merchants. They had an order for a crew to man the outward bound bark *Reaper*. The tug would take her lines at dawn and there was no time to waste.

An hour later the crimp's runner was back at the Blue Light or, more precisely, under it. He was seated in the stern of a big four-oared rowing boat that ghosted in through the barnacled piling that was the saloon's underpinning. The runner tapped the flooring above his head with a boat-hook's butt end, a trap door opened to flood the scummy harbor water with momentary light, revealing a haphazard pile of sprawled bodies between the thwarts of the boat. Then the body of young John Sutton came down to join the pile. The door slammed shut. A delivery had been made.

Next stop, the *Reaper,* lying deep-laden and lovely in the bay. Inert bodies hoisted aboard to go sprawling down the foc'sl hatch. Dull-gleaming gold pieces changing hands by the light of the flickering oil lamp in the skipper's cabin aft. A delivery had been completed.

The price was fifty dollars a body, which the *Reaper's* master considered a little high. Some years it dropped as low as thirty, but ships were thick in the bay and good hands were at a premium. Especially aboard the *Reaper . . . Grim Reaper,* the smart seamen called her, and spat when they said the name; and resolved to stay sober while she was seeking a crew, this bloody bucket, this hell-ship, this lousy, stinking, man-killing death wagon. . .

Which was strange, because the *Reaper* was a beautiful ship; a well-found, clean lined, lovely ship, and her captain was a kindly gentleman. All the *good* citizens of Port Townsend knew that, for he lived in a fine white house on the Bluff—on Captains' Row. He wore his high silk hat to church every Sunday, when he was ashore, and he gave money to the charities, and he patted children on the head when he passed them on the street . . . the clean well dressed children who lived on the Bluff.

But he had a first mate who wasn't a kindly man; a bucko mate named Hansen . . . Bully Hansen, who wasn't a kindly man at all. And Bully Hansen ran the ship. Drove the ship and the crew and made her

Above, top to bottom: Lumber schooners *Fearless, Vigilant, Fred E. Sander* and *C. S. Holmes.*

SCHOONERS, BARK

Left, top to bottom: *Forest Pride,* five-masted barkentine, leaving Grays Harbor. *Nokamish,* four-masted schooner, sailing into Port Townsend harbor under canvas. *Catherine Sudden,* three-masted barkentine, inbound with a full deck-load off San Francisco Bay. *Annie M. Campbell* in Commencement Bay, Tacoma.

Right, top to bottom: *Anne Comyn,* steel-hulled five-master, was one of the biggest of the lumber-carrying barkentines. *Samar,* four-masted topsail schooner, with cargo stowed, waiting to sail from Everett harbor. *Hawaii,* four-masted barkentine, squares away off Cape Flattery for trans-Pacific voyage.

AND BARKENTINES

Above, top to bottom: *Snow & Burgess* was a full-rigged ship when launched in 1878, later a bark and finally, as pictured here about 1905, a five-masted schooner. *Transit* was a typical four-master *Kiaulani* carried last lumber cargo from Grays Harbor under sail in 1940.

Right, top to bottom: *Albert,* three-masted wooden bark. *Skagit,* three-masted barkentine. *Blakely* was launched in 1877 as a 110-foot steam tug, was later converted to a sailing schooner and is pictured here about 1907 as a brig. *C. W. Clise* was posing for this 1899 photograph, with all sails, flags and the skipper's underwear flying in the breeze.

COQUILLE CITY WATERFRONT was an important Oregon lumber shipping point in the 1890's when this photograph was taken. Bar tug *Triumph,* left foreground, helped little two-masted lumber droughers like those at dock cross the tricky Coquille River bar. Stern-wheel steamboats carried freight and passengers on upper river.

Square-rigged ship *Santa Clara* loading full lumber cargo at Morrison Mill, Bellingham, 1916. (Lower left.)

Four-masted schooner *Ludlow,* a Hall Brothers product, at Port Blakely, 1900. (Lower right.)

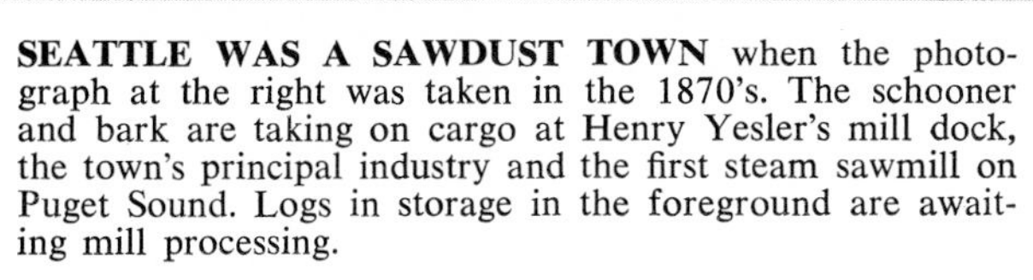

SEATTLE WAS A SAWDUST TOWN when the photograph at the right was taken in the 1870's. The schooner and bark are taking on cargo at Henry Yesler's mill dock, the town's principal industry and the first steam sawmill on Puget Sound. Logs in storage in the foreground are awaiting mill processing.

Everett was another major Puget Sound mill port. Sailing ships are pictured below loading in the harbor from scows and log booms.

TALL SHIPS AT ANCHOR were once a part of the seascape at Eagle Harbor, across Puget Sound from Seattle. This photograph was taken in post-World War 1 days when there were more sailing ships than lumber cargos. Many of the idle ships were destined for only one more voyage . . . to the shipbreakers' yards.

Five-masted schooner *George E. Billings,* opposite page, was one of the last and largest of the wooden ships built by Hall Brothers at Port Blakely. A 224-foot vessel of 1260 gross tons, she was launched in 1903, is pictured here on the Seattle waterfront.

pay her way. Bully Hansen was in high favor with the captain and all the owners of the ship for, among other economies he effected, his brutality usually drove the crews to desertion when a voyage was ended. In this simple fashion, the amount due them for wages was transferred to the owners' pockets.

It was Bully Hansen who brought young Sutton back to life; then made him wish he were dead again. Before that voyage was ended John Sutton got his wish. The *Reaper's* mate couldn't quite break this husky young logger's spirit so, in his simple, direct fashion, he broke his skull with a belaying pin. The

saloons that he'd sailed on the *Shenandoah* five years and "killed a man every trip." On the *Mary Flint* he hung a man up by the thumbs and left him there til he died. And on the *Reaper* a foremast hand once flung Hansen's curses back in his face. That man's tongue he cut out with his sailor's knife, leaving the body to drain its blood in the scuppers.

It was a shock to Bully Hansen when the police picked him up after the ship's return to San Francisco, a worse shock when he found himself sentenced to a stiff term in San Quentin Prison. Somehow John Sutton's story had spread beyond the waterfront, which is the only thing that made his case unique; his case or Bully Hansen's. The law, in those days which weren't so very long ago, seldom reached beyond the pierhead. Few profit-making bucko mates went to prison.

If you think such fiendish cruelty couldn't have happened in the American merchant marine in the twentieth century, consider the well documented case of a pair of seagoing sadists named Sparks and Watts, master and mate respectively of the American bark *Gatherer*.

Not one, but scores of sailormen were keelhauled from the hellship *Gatherer,* the process consisting of shipping a line from one side of the ship to the other, the bight of the line passing under the keel. The offending seaman, securely bound, was made

body, which had been valued at fifty dollars gold delivered on deck at Port Townsend, was shared by a group of cruising sharks somewhere north and west of the Solomon Islands.

There was nothing outstanding about the death of John Sutton. Mate Hansen prided himself on *always* killing at least one man each voyage. It kept the rest of the crew in line. He boasted in the waterfront

IDLE LUMBER SHIPS AT EAGLE HARBOR included the handsome barkentine *Forest Pride* in the foreground.

fast to one end of the line and thrown overboard to be hauled under the ship's keel and up on the other side. If one trip didn't drown or batter the unfortunate into submission, he went back over the same route.

It was on the *Gatherer's* voyage around the Horn to join the West Coast fleet at Townsend that the bloodiest chapter was added to her history. The bark had hardly cleared Sandy Hook when Watts started the process of "trimming" the shanghaied crew. This, in his book, meant beating every man aboard into a state of cringing servility, a process which he maintained with great relish all the way to San Francisco.

The first man went mad while the ship was beating around Cape Horn. One of the seamen who had been a special prey of the charming mate clawed his way aloft, screaming curses and defiance at the astonished Watts and, before the mate could grab a belaying pin, sprang overboard from the plunging upper topsail yard. The man at the helm involuntarily put the wheel down as the body plummeted into the sea, so Watts used the belaying pin on him, called for another helmsman, and leaned over the taffrail to watch the bobbing dot of humanity disappear in the gray, ice-cold seas astern.

The next incident to break the daily monotony of routine cuffs and kicks occurred when a German sailor was beaten into insensibility by Watts. As the man began to return to consciousness he gave vent to a muttered curse or two against the mate. Watts heard him, drew a revolver, and shot him through the head as he lay helplessly on the deck. Two seamen were ordered to dump the murdered German overboard. The body was hardly astern of the *Gatherer* when an A.B. named Swenson decided he'd had enough, too. He grabbed the sailmaker's knife, jumped to the rail, cut his own throat and toppled over into the sea.

Among the unfortunates of the *Gatherer's* foc'sl was the one man who had shipped voluntarily—a near-sighted college student who, poor devil, had thought the voyage would be good for his health! Watts, of course, broke his glasses for him the first day aboard, and from then on he was completely helpless. He couldn't even distinguish his friends of the foc'sl from the thuggish officers of the afterguard, and as a result he was a walking mass of welts and bruises.

Three days out of Frisco he bumbled into Watts' way again. The mate knocked him clear across the deck, where he lay in the scuppers, his face swelling like a purple balloon. When he came to and went blindly stumbling toward the foc'sl, he bumped Watts a second time. The mate knocked him down again, then drew a clasp-knife from his pocket and gouged out one of his eyes.

The young fellow lived in spite of his terrible injuries, and when, with the rest of the crew, he was kicked off the ship at San Francisco, he was met by several influential . . . and horrified . . . relatives.

Watts had made a serious mistake. He'd used his talents on somebody from "up town," and he went to Folsom Prison for a term of seven years.

Eagle Harbor drydock serviced schooners *Alice McDonald,* above, and *Resolute,* below, in sailing ship days.

TALL SHIPS O

Left, top to bottom: Brig *Mermaid* in Juan de Fuca Strait. Barkentine *Edward May* at San Francisco. Six-masted barkentine *Everett G. Griggs* towing in to Puget Sound. Schooner *Ruby* ready to sail from her Seattle pier.

Right, top to bottom: Topsail schooner *Monitor*. Five-masted barkentine *Monitor*. Three-masted barkentine *Newsboy* was built by Dickie Brothers of San Francisco in 1882. Unlike most West Coast-built lumber carriers, she bore a figurehead . . . a newsboy with a bundle of papers to commemorate the start in business of her first owner, J. J. Smith. She was operated by the Slade Lumber Company as a barkentine, was sold to Peruvian owners at start of World War 1.

HE TIMBER PORTS

Above, top to bottom: Barkentine *Irmgard,* built at Port Blakely in 1889, was later rerigged as three-masted schooner. *Lyman D. Foster* was a veteran of the Puget Sound-San Francisco lumber trade. *Wawona,* a graceful three-master, was built at Fairhaven, California in 1897 for the lumber trade, spent later years in the Bering Sea cod fisheries; is still afloat and in sailing trim at Seattle, although not in service for several years.

Right, top to bottom: *Crescent* spread fore-and-aft sails from five masts. *Mabel Gale,* pictured here crossing the Columbia River in tow of steamer *Wenona,* was a 183-footer built by Hall Brothers at Port Blakely in 1902. *Alex D. Brown* was built by T. C. Reed at Ballard (Seattle) in 1902 for Globe Navigation Co.; hauled lumber for Port Blakely Mill from 1915 until 1917, when she was wrecked in Australian waters. *Maggie Rugs* was photographed off Grays Harbor bar from coastal passenger steamer *Queen.*

GRACEFUL BARKENTINE BENICIA, named for the California port where she was built in 1899, led a colorful life in the offshore lumber trade until 1918, when she was sold to East Coast owners. After escaping many near disasters on the Pacific, she was finally wrecked off the coast of Haiti in 1920.

Captain Sparks stayed out of jail. He brought a number of character witnesses to court who all testified that the captain was a kindly gentleman who always wore his high silk hat to church when he was ashore, gave money to the charities, and patted children on the head. The jury apparently decided that such a kindly gentleman *couldn't* have known how Watts was carrying on.

It was the shanghai—the selling of doped and drunken men to windship masters—that produced and encouraged brutal killers like Watts and Bully Hansen, and there were many like them. Human life and human dignity comes cheap at fifty dollars a head, and after the crimps were paid their blood money it was economic to make life a hell for the human cattle they'd delivered. Cheaper to buy a new crew than to pay off the old one.

The practice originated in the days of the Saxon kings and continued as long as sailing ships fought the world's naval battles and carried the world's

FOUR-POSTER CAMANO, above, was one of the larger schooners built by Hall Brothers at Port Blakely in 1902, engaged in both offshore and coastwise lumber trade until after World War 1.

Bark *Vidette,* right, carried trans-Pacific lumber cargos for San Francisco owners.

commerce, but it got its name on the San Francisco Barbary Coast of the 1850's. "Sent to Shanghai," they said of unlucky seamen knocked on the head and hauled away to help fill the foc'sls of Orient-bound square-riggers, and the term has stuck.

The United States government proudly announced that the shanghai was a thing of the past when, in 1895, a law was passed requiring that the crew of a deepwater ship be signed on before the consul of the country whose flag it flew, or, if American, before a U.S. Shipping Commissioner. Only the signatures of men in full possession of their senses were to be accepted, and the signing had to be done in the presence of the government official.

It sounded fool-proof, but it wasn't. Few laws are when they try to put an end to a profitable industry. Fourteen years after the law was passed, in February of 1909 to be exact, the secretary of the British Foreign Sailors' Society in Vancouver had this to say about the methods employed in shipping offshore crews on Puget Sound:

"It costs ship owners on this (the Canadian) side $595 in blood money to purchase a crew of 17 men. It costs considerably more in ports on the American side. The price of sailors in Vancouver, New Westminster and Victoria today is $35 a man and the sellers are a well known American firm."

SURVIVOR OF A VANISHING BREED was the big schooner *Commodore,* built at Seattle in 1919. From 1923 until 1935 she sailed between Puget Sound and Hawaiian Islands, engaging in frequent races with the five-masted *Vigilant* owned by the same company, later sold to the Matson Navigation Company, her last service was in 1938 as a supply ship for an Alaska oil drilling company.

These detail scenes were taken aboard the *Commodore* during her last year in the offshore lumber trade.

BARKENTINE CONQUEROR, built at Rolph, California in 1918, had only one master, Captain James Hersey, who took command when she was commissioned and stayed with her until the end. After a long layup at Eagle Harbor following her last charter in 1928, Captain Hersey bought her from Hind Rolph & Company to save her from the junkyard. He and Mrs. Hersey lived aboard the *Conqueror* at Eagle Harbor for several years, but there were no more charters and he was finally forced to sell her.

Above, left, the *Conqueror* is pictured at temporary layup in Lake Union Seattle. At the center is a deck scene showing gear being stowed before her last voyage with a lumber cargo from Puget Sound to South Africa. Below she's pictured sadly awaiting cremation at a Seattle salvage yard.

FINAL HUMILIATION for many once beautiful sailing ships was reduction of status to that of a lowly barge or "unrigged vessel." Three such are pictured here, from top to bottom the former schooners *Wm. Nottingham, C. S. Holmes* and *Azalea.*

The melancholy contrast is dramatized by the picture on the opposite page of the *C. S. Holmes* in the heyday of her long career under taut canvas.

A well known firm, indeed, was the firm of Sims and Levy of Port Townsend, crimps to the Northwest sailing fleet. In 1906 the master of their sailors' boarding house—where their surplus stock was kept until the market was right—told a reporter for the Seattle *Times* that he was working for Port Townsend's most important industry.

"You see," he pointed out, "the town lives off the shipping. The customs house is here because of the shipping and the shipping is here because of Sims and Levy. They furnish the crews."

Then he delivered his clincher . . . "And furthermore, Sims and Levy don't never circulate less than two thousand bucks a month here in Port Townsend. That aint hay, friend, and the folks up on the hill know it."

The *Times* was interested in the activities of these affluent crimps because of a shocking affair that had taken place just off Seattle's fashionable watering place of Alki Point. A gasoline launch had come chugging up the Sound from the direction of Tacoma, an ambitious city which was running Port Townsend a close race for kidnapping honors. Off Alki Point, three young men were seen to dive overboard from the moving launch. One of them wasn't a very good swimmer and was hauled back aboard. The other two made it ashore.

The youngsters' names were Archie Cairns and Roy Phelps and they seemed mighty glad to see the helmeted cop who met them on the beach. They had just escaped, they said, from an attempt to shanghai them aboard the British square-rigger *Scottish Moors,* then lying in the stream off Seattle's waterfront.

The story made the newspapers, and it was quite a shock to the respectable people ashore who had been told that the government put the stopper on shanghaiing way back in 1895. But it seemed that it wasn't just a figment of the young men's imaginations. Federal authorities listened to their story and then put the pinch on the boarding house keeper and his runner who were transporting the boys to Seattle,

On the night of July 28, 1907 the Port Blakely-built four-masted schooner *Winslow*, two weeks out of San Francisco for Puget Sound, plunged headlong upon Duncan Rock with all sails set. She began filling immediately after striking the almost hidden reef to seaward of Cape Flattery. A boat was lowered and the crew, except for Captain Frederich and two men, put away from the ship. Although the decks were completely awash, the *Winslow* remained technically afloat throughout the night. At dawn the crew in the lifeboat returned and enough sail was reset to keep her off the Vancouver Island coast until the tug *Tacoma* arrived to tow the water-logged schooner to Seattle.

The photographs above and on the opposite page were taken as the *Winslow* lay in Elliott Bay awaiting a tow to the drydock at Eagle Harbor.

as well as the skipper and first mate of the *Scottish Moors*. The charge; abduction.

After that, more cases kept turning up. A 68-year-old man named Keating shanghaied aboard a lumber drougher at Townsend; a 15-year-old boy who went down to the waterfront for a look at the ships and didn't get home again. Then a house painter from inland Spokane named Charles Walker turned up with a story to tell.

Nine years before he had been slugged and robbed on a Spokane street, woke up in a box car rumbling across the Cascade Mountains toward tidewater. The car ended up in the yards at Tacoma, where a sympathetic stranger invited the battered Walker to have a cup of coffee with him. He woke up on board the Nova Scotian bark *Stillwater,* loaded with lumber and three days out at sea.

When he intimated to the skipper that he felt shanghaied, he was shown his signature on the shipping articles, a phenomena that puzzled him and might well have puzzled the lawmakers who had enacted the seamen's protective bill. He was probably lucky, at that. On an American ship he would probably have seen stars and comets instead of a fake signature when he made his protest. But they didn't beat you to death on a British ship. They starved you to death.

Arriving in South Africa after a 227 day voyage, Walker was so hungry that even army food looked good to him, so he signed up for a short hitch in a British regiment. The Boer War came along, turning his short hitch into a long one. Then he worked his way along the Cape Town to Cairo railway. Worked is the word; he had to help build it as he went along. From there he shipped to China, then to Australia, and from there he shipped to England as stoker on a White Star liner. Beating his way across Europe, he worked his way from Hamburg to Mexico on a sailing ship. He came back to Puget Sound on a coasting lumber schooner. The price of nine years of Charles Walker's life was thirty five dollars paid over to a Puget Sound crimp.

It was a sordid, bloody trade, and in the end it was profitable to nobody but the crimps. Shipmasters were robbed, along with the sailors they bought. Often a deal was made with a hard-pressed skipper, but when the tug was alongside his ship the crimps refused to deliver their human cargo aboard until the price was doubled. Nor was it uncommon for the runners, once having delivered a crew aboard, to return by night to kidnap them all over again for resale to another ship.

One of the most notorious of the Port Townsend runners was caught at this trick by the mate of a big British square-rigger and shot to death in the ensuing melee. Riots and mayhem were common on the waterfront and sometimes so noisy that the well-bred people on the Bluff had difficulty in ignoring them. But still the trade went on.

The skipper of the *William Nottingham* was carved half to death by a knife-wielding sailor who preferred the comforts of the penitentiary to the hardships of rounding the Horn in that lumber-laden schooner. An old man forcibly held aboard the *Guy C. Goss* secured a cleaver from the galley and hacked off several of his own fingers. But still the trade went on.

By the early years of the twentieth century it was limited to the West Coast, the last sanctuary of the windships, but it wasn't confined to Port Townsend. Up at Everett the Bucket of Blood Saloon was built over the Snohomish River, and had a trap door in the back room floor. Aberdeen, on Grays Harbor, and Astoria on the Columbia were almost entirely built over the water; trap doors and knock-out drops were not unknown there, nor in Portland, nor in San Francisco, where the custom got its name.

But they did it with a flair at Bloody Townsend, where you can still hear tales of the itinerant dentist who was partial to seafaring men. His sign said:

Sailors, Take Notice!

Remember, there are no dentists at sea! Don't start on a long voyage with bad teeth. Extractions guaranteed entirely painless!

When a ship was ready to sail and was still shorthanded, all his patients seemed to need extractions which were, indeed, quite painless. The dentist applied sufficient ether to keep them quiet until they could be delivered aboard ship and carried out to sea, where there was a good chance of their remaining molars being kicked out, painfully, by a bucko mate.

The trade ended, sometime after 1911—a 15-year-old boy is known to have escaped from a sailing vessel at San Francisco that year—but it wasn't ended by aroused public sentiment or by federal laws or by any of the other things that are supposed to stamp out abuses. Shanghaiing ended when there were no beautiful windships left to buy human bodies and make life a living hell for them.

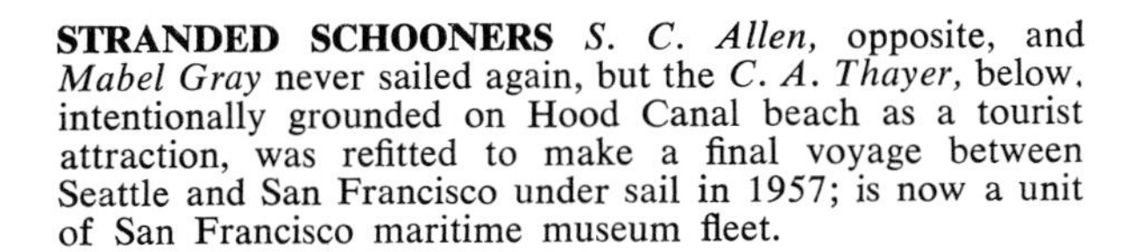

STRANDED SCHOONERS *S. C. Allen,* opposite, and *Mabel Gray* never sailed again, but the *C. A. Thayer,* below, intentionally grounded on Hood Canal beach as a tourist attraction, was refitted to make a final voyage between Seattle and San Francisco under sail in 1957; is now a unit of San Francisco maritime museum fleet.

Wreck of the ship *Jabez Howes,* above.

Wreck of the schooner *Janet Caruthers,* below.

Iron ship *Glenmorag* on the Oregon coast, above.

Schooner *Catherine Sudden* wrecked at Nome, below.

HIGH, DRY AND DESOLATE, the schooner *Oakland,* stranded on Neah-Kah-Nie Beach near Nehalem, Oregon in 1916, appeared to be a total loss. She was refloated. however, and carried West Coast lumber for another eight years until she sank off Cape Mendocino.

And when it ended, Port Townsend became a sleepy, respectable little ferryboat port. Today you can walk the length of Water Street without seeing a single saloon, and whatever painted women you meet are probably perfectly respectable, paint not being the distinguishing trade-mark that it was in 1900. You won't see many ships in the bay these days; none that are driven by sails. You probably won't be able to ship aboard one of them, no matter how much you'd like to, but if you do you'll make more money than most writers, you'll have a steam-heated room to yourself, and if the mate talks unkindly to you, you can report him to the union delegate.

The Shanghai Voyage isn't profitable any more, which is a wonderful thing except for Port Townsend. It's dull there nowadays.

THREE-MASTED TOPSAIL SCHOONER *Annie Larsen* was veteran West Coast lumber drougher.

TRIM FOUR-MASTER HELENE, built by Hall Brothers at Port Blakely in 1899, was pulled off at the next high tide after straying too close to the beach at Point Hudson, above, but the barkentine *Thos. P. Emigh,* Tacoma-built in 1902, was a total loss after stranding at Redondo Beach, California in 1932, below.

GRACEFUL BARKENTINES like the *James Tuft* were popular ships in the coastwise and offshore lumber trade.

SAD SENTINEL OF THE OREGON COAST, the remains of the British iron bark *Peter Iredale* have survived the inroads of sea, sand and rust since 1906, when she stranded south of the Columbia River entrance.

SCHOONER WILLIAM NOTTINGHAM, dismasted in a 1911 storm off the Columbia River, was refitted and made many more voyages. Her hull still lies on the beach at the mouth of the Nisqually River on upper Puget Sound.

Chapter 2

SCANDINAVIAN NAVY

THE steam schooner was a distinctive breed of ship peculiar to the American West Coast lumber trade. It evolved with simple forthrightness from the conventional lumber schooner when some astute ship owner decided that a boiler and steam engine of modest power would be a handy package to have aboard in case of emergency or calm.

Historians do not agree as to the first coastwise schooner to have a steam engine transplanted into her vitals. In California the *Beda, Alex Duncan, Newport, Surprise* and *Laguna* are all mentioned by authorities as deserving that honor. These little fore-and-afters were all converted to steam in the early 1880's and hundreds more were converted or constructed in the next half century.

Northwest maritime historians claim the steam schooner was actually born in their home waters years before the first San Francisco lumber droughers blossomed forth with smokestacks. The pioneer experimenter was Captain Jimmy Jones and the year was 1864.

Captain Jones had turned up on the West Coast during the California gold rush of 1849. He operated a small schooner out of San Francisco until 1858, when a new gold rush on the Fraser River of British Columbia beckoned him north. With the profits of this venture he built a new 95-foot schooner, the *Jenny Jones,* which he operated for a while as a conventional sailing vessel.

Jimmy Jones was a man of resource and imagination, however, and in 1864 he shanghaied an engine of sorts aboard the *Jenny Jones,* coupled it to a stout iron propeller, and proudly announced to dubious brother mariners that he was going to make a fortune running the *Jenny* between Portland and British Columbia ports. Since she was a *steam* schooner, he pointed out, he wouldn't need a towboat's help in getting up and down the Willamette River, nor would he be dependent upon the vagaries of wind and tide in getting across the Columbia River bar.

An admiring delegation of schoonermen went down to Astoria to watch the *Jenny Jones* make her epic first crossing of the bar under steam. An inshore wind was blowing and the tide was at flood, but Captain Jones jingled for full steam ahead and pointed the *Jenny's* blunt bows toward the open Pacific.

Steam schooner *Jane Nettleton*

At this point accounts differ. Some say the doughty captain was so proud of his success that he blew repeated blasts on the whistle, using up all the steam in the second-hand boiler; others have it that the temperamental engine simply broke down. At any event, the *Jenny Jones* found herself drifting toward the breakers with bare poles and no power. By the time the skipper was able to get sail up she was almost on the beach. He finally managed to get her back to Astoria, water-logged and battered, but the unfeeling laughter of his colleagues there further wounded his pride and dignity.

Perhaps Jimmy Jones has been generally overlooked as the true pioneer of the steam schooners because he was a Welshman and it is difficult to believe that anyone but a true Scandinavian deserves a place in the steam schooner hall of fame. Or per-

SEAGOING TEA KETTLE was what hardshell sailing skippers considered early steam schooners like the little *Point Loma,* above, but hundreds of the distinctive wooden lumber-carriers followed in her wake to "ride the breakers" of the Pacific Coast.

Steam schooners like Olson & Mahoney's 608-ton *J. Marhoffer,* opposite page, carried more cargo on deck than under hatches. The *Marhoffer,* built by Lindstrom at Aberdeen in 1907, stranded on the Oregon coast in 1910.

haps it is because the *Jenny Jones* led an unprofitable and somewhat disreputable career and ran away to Mexico pursued by angry U.S. Marshals. The story is told in Lewis and Dryden's *Marine History of the Pacific Northwest:*

"In February, 1865, he (Jones) became financially involved at Victoria and was thrown into jail. His schooner in the meantime had been sent to the American side in charge of the mate. The Victoria gaol, as they term it on that side of the line, was somewhat insecure and, through the intervention of friends, the captain secured a woman's dress and bonnet and escaped. After much trouble he landed on the American side of the Strait (of Juan de Fuca) only to learn that his steamer was in the hands of the United States marshal at Olympia, some of his American creditors having followed the example of the British Columbians.

"Captain Jones went to Olympia and, when the *Jenny Jones* was sent to Seattle to be sold, he went with her as a passenger. The vessel tied up for the night at Steilacoom and the marshal, not liking the quarters aboard, went to the hotel. After he retired 'Jimmy' decided upon a bold plan. With the United States Government against him on one side of the line and the British Government similarly interested on the other, with fuel only for a forty-mile run, a solitary sack of flour, two pounds of sugar and a pound of tea, he cast off the lines and steamed away.

"Before the hold was clear of wood he reached Port Ludlow, where he had previously located a few cords and, with the aid of this, he managed to reach Nanaimo (B.C.). Here he was refused coal but succeeded in obtaining a few provisions, steered for a deserted coal dump and engaged some Indians to assist him in getting aboard about twelve tons of coal dust which had been lying there for several years.

"With this supply he headed for the coast of British Columbia north of Burrard's Inlet to secure wood to mix with the coal dust, and when about twenty miles out encountered a leaky sloop with a cargo of provisions. The crew begged to be taken off

BOOMING MILL PORT OF ABERDEEN is pictured above in 1907. Behind the sailing vessels is a newly-built steam schooner being loaded with lumber, after which it will be towed to San Francisco by the smaller, white-hulled *Coronado* where engine and boilers will be installed. This was a common procedure in early-day steam schooner construction.

CONTRAST IN WOODEN SHIPS is provided, above, by the little steam schooner *George F. Haller,* foreground, and the square-rigged ship *Abner Coburn,* both typical of vessels used in coastwise and offshore lumber trade.

Below, left to right, the *Signal, South Coast* and *Jewel* were examples of the early lumber-carrying steam schooners built in 1887-8.

CONVERTED SAILING SCHOONER, the *Alcazar* was operated by L. E. White on the 14-hour run between his mill at Greenwood and San Francisco. She loaded cargo from wire cable chute below 150-foot cliffs. The *Alcazar* was stranded on Needle Rock in the summer of 1907.

the sinking craft, and he complied with the request and also did not neglect to secure their freight. Thus well manned and equipped the *Jenny Jones* struck out for the open sea and, with steam and sail both helping her down the coast, she arrived at San Blas after a journey of twenty five days. Here Jones paid the men their wages and also allowed them $625 for what he had taken from the sloop. He subsequently secured a profitable freight for Mazatlan and, on reaching that point, the crew again pressed him for money. 'Black Dutch' Albert of Port Townsend, one of the rescued, claimed $1000 and made application to the United States consul to have the steamer seized until his demand was acceded to. His evidence that she had run away after seizure was unsupported, however, and the vessel was released after paying the men.

"During the difficulty someone unshipped the rudder and secreted it and, becoming disheartened with continued annoyance, Jones sold the craft to the Mexicans for $10,000 and returned on the steamer *John L. Stephens* to San Francisco, where he was arrested but promptly discharged, the Court holding that according to the evidence the *Jenny Jones* had not left the marshal but the marshal had left her.

"After his return from the celebrated flight to foreign parts, he sailed the schooner *Discovery* for a Victoria firm for a short time, but finally became mentally unbalanced and traveled about the country giving lectures on the 'Eight Wonders of the World.' He died in Victoria, August 20, 1882, aged fifty two years."

At about the time poor Jimmy Jones, the unsung Welch pioneer of the Scandinavian Navy (his critics claimed he was lucky to be unhung) expired in Victoria, the first of hybrid San Francisco schooners were beginning to head north for lumber cargos. Equipped with little compound engines of a hundred horsepower or so, they spewed smoke from skinny stovepipe stacks and plowed along at a steady eight or nine knots, whether the wind was blowing or not.

Die-hard Scandinavian skippers grumbled that the stinkpot engines and bunkers wasted good cargo

FIRST OF THE McCORMICK STEAMSHIP COMPANY FLEET was the little *Cascade,* built by Hans Bendixsen at Fairhaven in 1904. In 1906, as larger steam schooners were added to the McCormick line, the *Cascade* was sold to Hawaiian owners.

space and the coal smoke dirtied up the sails, but even they took quiet enjoyment in passing up some still unconverted schooner lying-to for lack of wind. And it was certainly a comfort to know that when groping through a fog or poking into a rocky dog hole a signal to the engineer or his assistant, the "greaser," could stop her in a hurry.

A few ship owners were also reluctant to follow the new-fangled trend toward steam engines cluttering up honest lumber schooners. The Pope & Talbot interests, for years operators of the West Coast's biggest fleet of lumber carriers, never did make the transition to steam schooners. In 1916 the remnants of the once great sailing fleet, the schooners *Camano, Gamble, Okanogan* and *Spokane,* were sold to Balfour Guthrie and the P. & T. house flag was furled for more than three decades.

Most coastwise operators were impressed with the performance of the sailing schooners with steam engines, however, and by the late 1880's the San Francisco machine shops and boiler works were flooded with orders as smokestacks blossomed from the sterns of dozens of the little ships which had formerly relied only on the wind for power.

The first vessel to be built originally as a steam schooner was a modest little craft of 218 tons which was launched at the San Francisco yard of Boole & Beaton in 1888. Christened the *Newsboy,* she had been ordered by a tall Scotch-Canadian mill owner from Northern California, Robert Dollar by name. The 129-foot *Newsboy* went to work carrying cedar logs and passengers between Eureka and San Francisco, her skinny black funnel emblazoned with a red band bearing a white $-sign. It was an insignia destined to become well known on most of the world's seven seas.

The *Newsboy* herself led a fairly uneventful life for a steam schooner, although she did make several hazardous voyages from Seattle to Nome during the Alaska gold rush, her cramped decks heaped with amazing amounts of freight and peopled by a good many more passengers than she could comfortably accommodate. After this service she was sold to the Merchants' Independent Steamship Company and,

"BUG BOAT" OF FRED LINDERMAN'S "INSECT LINE" was the little wooden steam schooner *Bee,* above, her modest size contrasted with the bulk of the Japanese trans-Pacific steamer in the background. The *Helen P. Drew,* below, wasn't much bigger than the tug *Sea Ranger* docked just astern. The *Drew,* built by G. H. Hitchings at Hoquiam, was towed to Greenwood, picked up a redwood tie cargo and then proceeded to San Francisco where her machinery was installed by Fulton Iron Works.

NAMED FOR THE TOP TYCOON OF THE LUMBER FLEET, the *Charles Nelson,* above, was a 630-tonner, built by Hay & Wright at Alameda in 1898. Designed to carry a few passengers, she crammed hundreds aboard when the government took her over as an army transport during the Spanish-American War. She made several voyages to the Philippines carrying uncomfortable soldiers, then returned to the lumber trade until 1910, when she caught fire and burned to the waterline in Humboldt Bay. Her engines went into the new Nelson steam schooner *Mukilteo,* her hull was converted to a lumber barge.

The 208-ton *Newsboy* of 1888 vintage was the forerunner of the present-day line of American President liners. She sank in collision with the steam schooner *Wasp* on Humboldt Bay in 1906.

ROUGH SEAS AND BREAKING BARS made tough going for the small wooden ships of the coastwise lumber fleet. The *Tillamook,* above, was an unusual type, built along typical steam schooner lines, but powered by a 280-horsepower gas engine. Built at North Bend, Oregon in 1911, she's pictured bucking her way across the Bandon River bar.

HIGH-PILED DECKLOADS like that on the *Vanguard,* left, usually made the coastwise voyage to the California lumber market safely. Sometimes high seas and winter winds opened seams and scattered deckloads, however, as in the case of the *Daisy Freeman,* below.

NO STRANGERS TO THE BEACH were the steam schooners of the "Scandinavian Navy," but it was hard to keep them there. The *Tamalpais,* a 1906 product of Matthews' Hoquiam yard, was beached after striking on Blunt's Reef in 1913, but was pulled off and survived until 1931. McCormick's *Everett,* one of the largest of the wooden steam schooners, was quickly refloated after going ashore between Seattle and Tacoma in 1926, but she foundered a few months later off Table Bluff, California.

in April of 1903, was reported as 35 hours overdue on the 40-hour run from San Pedro to San Francisco. Apparently her new owners followed Captain Dollar's custom of overloading the poor little *Newsboy,* for she was said to be carrying "14 first-class passengers and 18 second-class passengers, besides a crew of 20 and a large amount of freight." She eventually made port this time, but on another April three years later she was butted by the steam schooner *Wasp* and sank in Humboldt Bay.

Although her original owner, Robert Dollar, was nearly sixty years old when he embarked with her in the shipping business, he knew a good thing when he saw it and wasted no time in expanding both his lumber and shipping interests. As his markets extended to the Far East, shipping gradually replaced lumber as his major interest and he expanded his trans-Pacific freighter service, acquired an interest in the Pacific Steamship Company and methodically prepared for a major entry into the passenger business. This he made in 1923 with the acquisition of seven "502" type passenger liners from the United States Shipping Board, and, a year later, of five larger "535" type ships. In 1924 one of these ships, the *President Harrison,* departed on the first round-the-world voyage of an American-flag passenger ship. (The *Diana Dollar* had followed the same course two years earlier to become the first American freighter to circle the globe.)

Robert Dollar was an exponent of the *laissez faire* philosophy of business and his ships were known for the scant fare dished up to crews. He violently opposed the LaFollette Seamen's Bill of 1915, putting his fleet under British registry for a time after it was passed. He took considerable pride in having broken up the San Francisco waterfront strike of 1910 by organizing goon squads who were tougher and more violent than the strikers. He also promised to personally lynch the mayor unless civic action was taken against the strikers.

At the age of 81 he took time out from peering at ledgers and poking into corners at his mills, logging camps and ships to make the grand tour around the world on one of his own President liners. After the old man's death his shipping empire was beset by hard times and the government took over its operation for a time, but ever since that voyage of the *President Harrison* in January of 1924, President liners have been steaming east to west around the globe, the only such service in the world operating under one house flag. When American President Lines celebrated the thirtieth anniversary of this service in 1954, President liners had completed 600 voyages around the world . . . an equivalent distance of 31 trips to the moon and back.

"From Newsboy to President" is a fitting title for the story of the great steamship line which had its beginnings in 1888 with the launching of the first of the Pacific Coast's "ready-made" steam schooners.

The American President Lines is not the only major present-day steamship company which can trace its start to a single little wooden steam schooner. Back in 1901 a young man named Charles R. McCormick arrived in Portland from the East, quickly obtaining a job as sales manager for the Hammond Lumber Company which operated its own fleet of steam schooners to haul the 40 million feet of lumber its mills produced each year. McCormick was a good salesman, but he hadn't come West to work for somebody else. By 1903 he was in partnership with Sidney Hauptman operating a small redwood shingle mill at Eureka and lumber brokerage firm in San Francisco.

The firm was so short on cash that when they secured their first large brokerage order . . . for 400,000 feet of redwood lumber to be delivered from Humboldt Bay to San Pedro . . . they had to borrow money to charter a little two-masted schooner from the Pacific Lumber Company at a rate of four dollars per thousand feet. After paying this fee, along with other expenses, the partners found they had made a profit of fifty cents a thousand on their lumber compared to the four dollars a thousand the schooner's owners had received.

OLD-TIMERS OF THE STEAM SCHOONER FLEET were the *National City,* upper left, built at San Francisco in 1888 and sold to Peruvian owners in 1918, and the *Cleone,* also built at the Bay City in 1887. The *Cleone* was an early command of Captain "Hoodlum Bob" Walvig, gained later fame for the lugubrious sound of her whistle. The *Cleone* is pictured on the opposite page above a bit of immortal steam schooner poetry written in her honor by a bard whose name, unfortunately, has not been recorded.

THE MOAN OF THE "CLEONE"

A long drawn wail, a cough, a sigh, disturbs our rest at night
While stout hearts curse the author, and weak ones cower in fright;
Some said it was a cow in pain, or that Mac had cut a hog
But creeping up the Bay we saw, 'twas Whistling Eddie Skog.

The Cleone's speed is five knots straight, in calm and pleasant weather,
But with head wind she goes astern, or else stops altogether.
When her whistle blows, her steam runs down and so she loses way
And thus is several hours late, on her passage either way.

To Uncle Hans it's bliss divine to hear that doleful cry;
He'd cock his ear, and spread his wings as down the hill he'd fly.
With a stream of Swede and a word or two that none could understand
He sure thought Whistling Eddie was the noblest in the land.

The Moonshine outfits in the hills, would quiver at the sound;
The Crabs would bark, the Clams forsake their favorite feeding grounds.
The Hens would crow, the cows would squeal, and so would every dog;
At the passing of the Cleone and Whistling Eddie Skog.

The Cleone's lines are sweet and true, she is a noble craft;
With one Mast stuck up foward, and nothing stuck up aft.
And with her load of logs on deck, about four ricks or less;
But when her awful whistle blows, we fear she's in distress.

We hope that good old Santa Claus, will note our fearful plight;
And put a horn in Eddie's sock, when he hangs it up at night.
For then we'll lie in bed in peace and breathe a silent prayer;
As the Cleone's horn to us is borne, on the still and ambient air.

In the book of regulations, for steam boats on the Sea;
He will find a section of the law laid down for such as he.
That "unnecessary whistling shall in no way be allowed"
But of "Cleone's" consumptive cough, Capt. Skog is strangely proud.

Please take a tumble Eddie, and strive to make amends;
Don't split the ear drums of your Foes and likewise of your friends.
Give rest unto the Clams and Cow, the Chickens and the Hog;
So that all may shower their blessings on Commander Eddie Skog.

. . . Author unknown

ONE OF THE FIRST OF THE DOUBLE-ENDED STEAM SCHOONERS, the *Daisy Mitchell,* pictured here loading at Aberdeen, was built in 1905 by Bendixsen for S. S. Freeman. A radical departure from conventional steam schooner design of that era, she had engines, deckhouses and passenger accommodations amidships, a feature which was incorporated in many of the later lumber carriers.

It became obvious to McCormick, as it had to Pope and Talbot more than half a century earlier, that the best way to make money on a cargo of lumber was to own the vessel upon which it was shipped. Accordingly he consulted with his friend Captain Ed Jahnsen, veteran master of the Hammond steam schooner fleet, who conducted him to Fairhaven and the shipyard of Hans Bendixsen. On the ways lay a neat little steam schooner, partially completed. Bendixsen was building her on speculation and she was for sale. McCormick handed over $15,000, which was every dime he had in the world, and signed a note for the balance of $45,000 on completion.

The more conservative partner, Hauptman, took a dim view of this transaction, but McCormick enthusiastically formed the Cascade Steamship Company and began selling stock . . . sixty four shares at $1062.50 each. Stockholders eventually included ship chandlers, grocers, insurance brokers and even the shipwrights who were working on the new steam schooner *Cascade*. Everyone who came within range of Charles McCormick's persuasive voice and possessed the sum of $1062.50 became an investor, with the result that Bendixson was paid off and an engine was purchased from the Fulton Iron Works.

Late in December of 1904 the *Cascade* sailed on her maiden voyage well loaded down with 550,000 feet of lumber and under the capable command of Captain Jahnsen. By the time she was sold six years later she had earned her purchase price and made an annual profit of ten per cent besides, and by 1910 McCormick had added the steam schooners *Klamath, Shoshone, Yellowstone* and *Yosemite* to his fleet. These were soon joined by the *Celilo, Willamette, Multnomah, Ernest H. Meyer, Everett,*

BUILT FOR PASSENGERS' COMFORT, steam schooners of the McCormick fleet were popular with coastwise travelers. The *Multnomah,* built at St. Helens in 1913, demonstrates the larger space devoted to passenger accommodations on the more modern wooden lumber carriers. The 970-ton *Multnomah* was wrecked off the Columbia River bar in the summer of 1929.

Wahkeena and *Wapama.* Many of these ships, as well as those of other operators, were built at McCormick's own St. Helena Shipbuilding Company located just above the junction of the Willamette and Columbia Rivers. The *Multnomah,* launched in October, 1912, was the first of 42 vessels to be built there in the next fifteen years.

All of the McCormick steam schooners carried passengers as well as lumber cargoes and, in 1924 the coastwise passenger liners *Rose City* and *Newport* went under the McCormick house flag. By 1925 the company was operating 71 vessels between 23 Pacific Coast ports from Canada to Mexico. The passenger-carrying steam schooners were a great convenience to the citizens of the smaller coastal ports where the regular passenger liners didn't call and the McCormick ships, with their distinctive star-shaped funnel markings, achieved an enviable record of regular service, dependability and good cuisine.

Eventually McCormick extended operations to the intercoastal trade and to South America, besides taking over control of that original giant of the Northwest lumber industry, Pope & Talbot's Puget Mill Company. By the beginning of the second world war the McCormick Steamship Company was operating a fleet of more than twenty five steel ships in coastwise, intercoastal and South American trade.

By 1940, however, it was evident that McCormick had over extended his operations and most of the McCormick interests reverted to a reorganized Pope & Talbot corporation, this firm operating the McCormick fleet for the government during the war years. After 1946 the steamship division of Pope & Talbot lost little time in replacing the old McCormick ships with a fleet of six 12,000-ton C-3 type freighters and one 10,000-ton Victory type.

The traditional McCormick "M" has disappeared from the funnels of the big post-war freighters,

MC CORMICK STEAMSHIP CO.

Above, top to bottom: *Celilo,* 943-ton McCormick liner, built at St. Helens, 1913; abandoned Oakland Creek, 1931. *Wahkeena,* 1030 tons, built by Wilson Brothers at Astoria, 1917; stranded near Grays Harbor, 1929. *Shoshone,* 646 tons, built by Bendixsen at Fairhaven in 1908. Later sold to Hawaiian owners and renamed *Hamakua.*

Right, top to bottom: *Ernest H. Meyer,* 1057 tons, was built at St. Helens in 1917, was destroyed by fire in 1930. *Klamath,* 1038 tons, was built by J. H. Price at Fairhaven in 1910, stranded at Del Mar Landing, California in 1921. *Yosemite,* 827-tonner built by Bendixsen in 1906, stranded at Point Reyes in 1936. *Wapama,* pictured here in her old age as the *Tongass,* 951 tons, built at St. Helens in 1915, has been completely restored and, under her original name, is on permanent exhibit by the San Francisco marine museum.

HART-WOOD LUMBER CO.

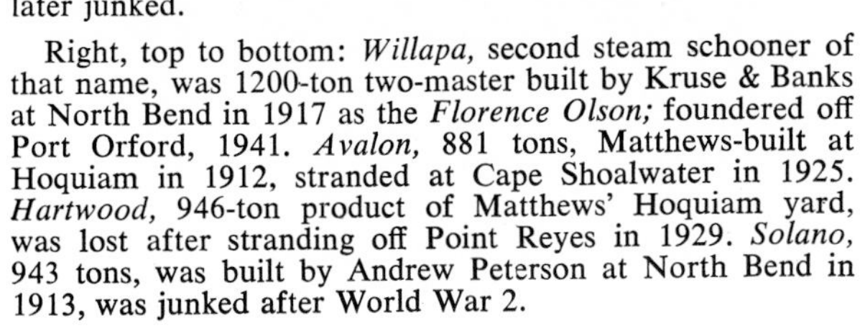

Above, top to bottom: *Quinault* (1) was 580-ton "stem-winder" built by John Lindstrom at Aberdeen in 1906; stranded at Punta Gorda, 1917. *Quinault* (2) was 1138-ton "double-ender" built by Matthews at Portland in 1921; was in service until after World War II. *Claremont,* 1290 tons, built at Hoquiam by Matthews in 1917 was later renamed *Alwill* and *North Bend.* Broken up after World War 2. *San Diego,* 1500 tons, was a giant of the wooden steam schooner fleet. Built by Matthews at Portland in 1918, she was abandoned on Oakland Creek during depression years, later junked.

Right, top to bottom: *Willapa,* second steam schooner of that name, was 1200-ton two-master built by Kruse & Banks at North Bend in 1917 as the *Florence Olson;* foundered off Port Orford, 1941. *Avalon,* 881 tons, Matthews-built at Hoquiam in 1912, stranded at Cape Shoalwater in 1925. *Hartwood,* 946-ton product of Matthews' Hoquiam yard, was lost after stranding off Point Reyes in 1929. *Solano,* 943 tons, was built by Andrew Peterson at North Bend in 1913, was junked after World War 2.

but Pope & Talbot's "P-T" is superimposed on the same five-pointed white star that one graced the stack of the Charles McCormick's diminutive steam schooner *Cascade*.

Other shipping tycoons of the colorful steam schooner era, like the builders of the little ships, did not survive the transition from wood to steel. There was Fred Linderman, whose real ambition in life was to own a little California farm where he could raise bees. When fate dealt him a fleet of steam schooners instead he compromised by giving them such names as *Bee, Wasp, Hornet* and *Cricket*. The last of Linderman's "bug boats," the steel steam schooner *Cricket* was, at last reports, still plying the waters of the Pacific under Mexican ownership, but the rest have vanished, along with all the rest of the wooden lumber ships.

During the depression years of the 1930's, with the lumber market in the doldrums and the era of the wooden steam schooner almost ended, Linderman substituted "salad barges" for his timber-toting "bug boats." Like many big cities, Oakland was having trouble getting rid of its garbage and the "salad barges" were the old steam schooners *Tahoe* and *Hoquiam* with garbage bunkers installed on their decks which, in better days, had been fragrant with the aroma of western cedar, Douglas fir and redwood. Each morning one of the pair, laden with 600 tons of refuse, would wend its odiferous way through the Golden Gate and out to the dumping area off the Farallones. The *Tahoe* and *Hoquiam* were not popular with the residents of other coastal cities in the Bay area, who complained bitterly that their beaches were festooned with Oakland garbage after every high tide. Even their crews were not happy. Jack McNairn and Jerry MacMullen, in their delightful steam schooner saga, *Ships of the Redwood Coast,* describe the poignant plea of respectable steam schooner skippers reduced to piloting maritime garbage wagons:

"Freddie, vy don' you giff oop diss idea? My vife, she say I got to stay on de ship if ve go on hauling svill. She say I shtink—und, py Yesus, she iss right! Giff it oop Freddie! Let's haul shingles, und not garbage!"

Oliver Olson was another steam schooner mogul who started business with an idea and 64 blank stock certificates, of which he could only afford to purchase one. When a friend of his named Jim Butler came to town from the Nevada mines with enough money to buy up the unsold stock and put the firm in business the name *Jim Butler* was gratefully painted on the bows of the steam schooner building at John Lindstrom's Aberdeen yard. The *Jim*

Butler, later renamed *Crescent City,* started hauling lumber for Oliver Olson in 1906; was soon joined by the Lindstrom-built *Thomas L. Wand.*

Olson's timing was excellent, for that was the year of the great San Francisco earthquake and fire. The coastal lumber fleet was hard-pressed to supply the lumber needed to rebuild the city and freight rates were high. Olson needed more ships and was scouring San Francisco for the needed funds when he met Andy Mahoney, a shoe salesman who had just won $15,000 on a lottery ticket. Mahoney wanted to get into the shipping business and Olson was in a mood to accommodate him, reaching for the bankroll with his left hand and shaking the lucky shoe salesman's hand with his right. Thus was formed one of the West Coast's most spectacular shipping partnerships.

Norwegian Olson and Irish Mahoney indulged in frequent clashes of temperament and it was said that their arguments were clearly audible for a distance of half a mile against the wind. Olson's rage reached a crescendo when he returned from an Eastern business trip to discover that Mahoney had decided to have the hulls of the company's ships painted a bright shamrock green. Unable to find words to express his displeasure, he retaliated by having a single huge letter "O" painted on the stack of each green-hulled Olson & Mahoney steam schooner.

Mahoney was in no position to say anything about the omission of his initial from the firm's funnel marking and it remained that way even before 1916, when Andy Mahoney sold out his interest in the steam schooner fleet. The Oliver J. Olson Company, as the line was then renamed, survived the change

Right, top to bottom: *San Ramon,* 993 tons, built at North Bend in 1913, was operated by Sudden & Christenson. *Helen P. Drew,* 309 tons, built by G. H. Hitchings at Hoquiam in 1904 and operated by White Lumber Co., ended her days on the mudflats at Martinez. *Katherine,* 531 tons, was built by John Lindstrom at Fairhaven in 1908, operated by Redwood Steamship Co.; burned in 1940. *James H. Higgins,* Higgins Lumber Co., 550-ton "stem-winder" was stranded at Point Hueneme, California in 1916.

Left, top to bottom: *F. S. Loop,* 794 tons, built by Kruse & Banks at Marshfield, Oregon in 1907 for Loop Lumber Co., was sold to Mexican owners and converted to gas-powered barge. *Grace Dollar,* 429 tons, built by Fulton Iron Works at San Francisco in 1898 was originally named *Hardy.* After serving Robert Dollar's Usal, California mill was renamed *San Antonio.* Final disposition unknown. *Willamette* (2), 900 tons, built by Bendixsen in 1911 was once victim of armed pirates on San Francisco-Seattle run. Renamed *California* and, later, *Susan Olson,* she was converted to a floating fish fertilizer plant; foundered off Port Orford in 1941. *Daisy Matthews,* 943 tons, built by Matthews at Hoquiam for Freeman Lumber Co., foundered off Trinidad Head, 1940.

TYPICAL "STEM-WINDER" of the West Coast steam schooner fleet was the little *San Pedro* pictured here plowing up San Francisco Bay with cargo booms rigged and ready to begin discharging high-piled cargo of Grays Harbor lumber.

from wooden to steel coasters, substituting motor cranes in recent years for the old-style oversize cargo booms of the traditional lumber schooners. Under the direction of Olson's sons, George and Whitney, the firm has become the last of the more than a hundred companies that operated coastwise steam schooners in the glory days of the lumber fleet.

The steam schooner skippers were at least as colorful as the rugged individualists they worked for and the imaginative nicknames they bore. Hit-the-Bar Hansen spent most of his maritime career sailing steam schooners out of Grays Harbor, with his son as mate. He maintained a neat shoreside home in Aberdeen and the neighbors always knew when Captain Hansen and his son left home for another voyage. At the gate he would turn and loudly shout, "Gootby, mama! Ve see you in a couple veeks . . . if ve don't hit da bar!"

This parting word was always delivered with loud bellows of laughter to make it clear that this was only a family joke, for Captain Hansen was far too skilled and experienced a skipper to come to grief on the Grays Harbor bar.

But, alas, one early morning the voice of Captain Hansen was heard crying dolefully in the pre-dawn darkness as he stood dripping wet on his front porch.

"Come down und let us in, mama. *Ve hit da bar!*"

Another Grays Harbor skipper bore the unflattering title of Henpecked Jorgenson. His wife, apparently embittered by a crippling accident which made it necessary for her to use a crutch, made the captain's shoreside stays so tough on him that he always looked forward joyfully to sailing day. Even these had their tribulations, however, for his wife would accompany him to the dock, berating him all the way. If he dared to talk back she was likely to whack him briskly over the head with her crutch.

This went on for years, until Mrs. Jorgensen finally demanded that her husband take her with him on one of his coastwise voyages. Needless to say, she won her point and on sailing day the crew could hear her coming several blocks away as she shrilly scolded her unhappy husband.

She continued her tirade all the way up the gangplank and into the saloon, but as he felt the familiar deck of the steam schooner under his feet a strange

HUMILIATING OLD AGE was the fate of many of the wooden steam schooners when their timber-hauling days were over. The sturdy hulls were converted to such diverse uses as fish reduction plants, floating canneries, fertilizer factories and garbage barges. Here the *Chatham* is pictured on the way to becoming an Alaska fish processing plant.

transformation came over the henpecked captain. He suddenly straightened his stooped shoulders, thrust out his jaw, turned his amazed wife over his knee and began thrashing her soundly with her own crutch.

"Py Yesus!" he shouted between whacks, "She don't treat me dis vay on my own boat!"

Legend has it that Mrs. Jorgenson completed the voyage in a ladylike manner and was, from that day forward, a dutiful and obedient wife both afloat and ashore.

Captain Anderson, who first commanded little steam schooners for Robert Dollar and later became commodore of the Dollar Line fleet of globe-circling President liners was one of the first of the coastwise lumber skippers to try his hand at navigating a horseless carriage. He purchased one of the early Model-T Fords and was given driving lessons by the salesman, as was the custom in those days. Captain Anderson was too old a dog to learn new tricks, though, and he persisted in driving his Ford as if he were handling a steam schooner.

One Seattle waterfront old-timer recalls making a land voyage with the captain in his Model-T, in the course of which his right-of-way was challenged by two boys on a bicycle.

"Hang on!" the skipper bellowed, "there's a bicycle crossing our bows and I'm gonna swing her hard t'starboard!"

Since he put the same muscular action into play to turn the Ford as was required to swing 'round a 600-ton steam schooner, his warning was needed. As the bicycle zipped past the shuddering Ford the captain leaned outboard, shook his fist and roared, "Sheer off there, you hayseeds! Sheer off I say!"

Captain Charles Reiner, veteran McCormick steam schooner master and holder of the Congressional Life Saving Medal had his courage put to an unusual test during the course of what should have been a routine coastwise voyage. His steam schooner, the *Willamette,* had pulled away from her San Pedro pier on the evening of December 30, 1913, bound

STEAM SCHOONER ALBUM

Left, top to bottom: *Coaster,* 579 tons, built by Lindstrom at Aberdeen in 1905, was later renamed *Caoba;* wrecked off the Columbia River in 1925, her hull was driven ashore near Ocean City, Washington, where her rusty boiler still rests in the sand. *G. C. Lindauer,* 453 tons, also Aberdeen-built by John Lindstrom, in 1901, was stranded near the Umpqua River mouth in 1924. *Rochelle,* built on the Great Lakes in 1896 was originally a type of fresh-water vessel akin to the West Coast steam schooner and called a "lumber hooker" by lake sailors. She was brought west and rebuilt as a steam schooner. *Chehalis,* 633 tons, built by Bendixsen at Fairhaven in 1901, and operated by Sudden & Christenson until laid up on the Oakland mudflats.

Above, top to bottom: *J. B. Stetson,* 837 tons, was built at Winslow, Washington in 1905 as the *Cornell;* stranded on the California coast in 1934. *Florence Olson,* 1185 tons, built for Olson and Mahoney at North Bend, Oregon, was renamed *Willapa* (2) when transferred to McCormick ownership. Foundered off Port Orford, 1941. *Yellowstone,* 767-ton Bendixsen-built steam schooner of 1907 vintage was early unit of McCormick fleet; foundered in Humboldt Bay in 1933.

STEAM SCHOONER ALBUM

Above, top to bottom: *Fair Oaks* was originally the *Robert Dollar,* an 800-ton "double-ender" built at Hoquiam in 1900; was transferred to East Coast service during World War 1. *Navarro,* 232 tons, built by Hay & Wright at San Francisco in 1887 was another of the very early coastwise steam schooners. *San Jacinto,* 614 tons, was built by Matthews at Hoquiam in 1908. Later renamed *Border King,* she carried general cargo between Puget Sound and British Columbia ports. Sold to Greek owners and under Panamanian registry, renamed *Mario,* she was wrecked on the Cuban coast in 1944.

Right, top to bottom: *Argo* was a tiny timber-toter of 210 tons, built at Ballard (Seattle) in 1898. *Alex Duncan* was originally a sailing schooner. This photograph, taken at San Francisco in 1883, backs claims of some marine historians that she was first lumber schooner to be converted to steam. (Note furled sails on both masts.) *Salina Cruz* was new name of the old *Anne Hanify* after she was sold to Mexican owners. Built by Kruse & Banks at North Bend, she burned at sea off Grays Harbor in 1949. *Daisy Gray,* 1187 tons, Portland-built by Matthews in 1923, was the last wooden steam schooner ever launched. She remained in service until after World War 2.

WORKING ALL HOLDS with typical long-reaching cargo booms, Hart-Wood's big (1300-ton, 225-foot) *Claremont* (2) was gobbling up carloads of dimension lumber at Willapa Harbor dock when this 1937 picture was taken. Launched at the Hoquiam yard of the Matthews Shipbuilding Company in 1917, she was powered with a 900-horsepower triple-expansion engine.

Barbara C., left, was built as the *Pacific* by Kruse & Banks at North Bend in 1920; was operated until about 1945 by W. R. Chamberlin Company.

Opposite page: *Border King,* ex-*San Jacinto,* at Borderline Transportation Company dock on the Seattle waterfront. Lower right, *Hartwood* loading at Olympia, 1927.

for San Francisco and Puget Sound. The ensuing drama, which had its overtones of slapstick comedy, was reported as follows by the San Francisco newspapers of January 2, 1914:

"A sea rover and Arctic trader turned pirate, A. B. Nelson, himself master mariner and one time owner of the schooner *Hera,* was today brought to port in irons, locked in the brig of the steam schooner *Willamette* and turned over to the federal authorities who held him in $10,000 bail on charges of assaulting Captain Reiner on the high seas with intent to murder.

"With him was brought Joseph Laramie, bricklayer, who says he is from Shelby, Ind., charged with being an accomplice in the crime. He was held in the same bail. Neither man will admit that he knows the other.

"Nelson was arrested Wednesday night after a hand to hand battle in the captain's cabin, which he had entered muffled in a towel, wearing a brown wig as thick as a thatch and as palpably false, a false mustache and carrying an automatic 44-calibre pistol in his outstretched hand.

"Although a smaller, lighter man, Captain Reiner fought the pistol away from the grotesque pirate,

...AND MORE DECKLOADS

THERE WERE NO PLIMSOLL MARKS ON THE LUMBER SCHOONERS and the cargo was stacked aboard until the skipper was convinced that another sling of two-by-fours might sink her. Hart-Wood Lumber Company's 747-ton first *Claremont,* above, had a five-foot freeboard and twelve-foot deckload when this photograph was taken in 1910.

The poles of the *Andy Mahoney's* deckload were destined for Mexico, where they were cut into props for the underground tunnels of the Santa Rosalia mines.

THE BEST LAID DECKLOADS went oft a'rie when subjected to the full force of a North Pacific storm. The *Santa Monica,* above, ran into a southwester off Cape Flattery in the winter of 1907 which broke her deckload lashings and sent her back to Puget Sound to pull herself together again, assisted by the tug *Alice.*

Loose and shifting deckloads sometimes gave storm-battered ships a dangerous list. The *Davenport,* below, made it back to the shelter of Neah Bay inside Cape Flattery, but others weren't always as fortunate.

TOPPING OFF THE DECKLOAD

Longshoremen load the final slingloads of Puget Sound lumber aboard an intercoastal freighter as an offshore carrier enters port in ballast, ready to take aboard a five million foot cargo for trans-Pacific shipment.

MORE DECKLOADS, as carried by the *Coronado,* left, built at Aberdeen in 1900 as the first "double-ended" steam schooner, the *Rainier,* built at Hoquiam later the same year, the steel *Lake Francis* and the *Centralia,* opposite page top, the steel steam schooner *Henry T. Scott,* opposite page center, and McCormick's big three-islander *Peter Helms,* opposite page lower.

who immediately drew a double action 44-calibre revolver. He was getting the better of the captain when two sailors and a waiter rushed into the room, overpowered Nelson and ironed him. Laramie was standing outside the door while the fight was in progress. The *Willamette* carried $1500 in cash to pay the crew of 25 and there were 25 passengers quartered aft.

"A launch followed the vessel, keeping distant about half a mile for some time and Captain Reiner believes the pirate intended to rob the ship's safe, hold up the passengers for their cash and valuables and make his escape to shore in the launch. Elaborate notations of possible landing places, giving distance and compass bearings, were found in his clothes.

"After turning over his prisoner and telling his tale, Captain Reiner put out to sea again, bound for Seattle. He would not be alive tonight were it not that in fighting for possession of the pistol he was lucky enough to put the mechanism out of order.

The pirate was pulling the trigger constantly until he realized that the weapon was useless, when he threw it on the floor and drew his revolver.

"So terrifying an apparition did he make in his mask and wig that the captain's nephew, a lad of 17, burst from the room and ran headlong to the forecastle where, inarticulate with fright, he fell in a dead faint before he could make known his uncle's plight. It was the noise of the scuffle that finally drew the crew to the captain's aid.

"Nelson is a shabbily dressed, hulking lump of a man, with blonde hair, thinning above the temples, clean shaven and looking all the 35 years he owns. His manner is stolid, but he talked rapidly enough.

" 'I'm a private detective,' he said. 'There's a reward of $10,000 for the capture of Captain Reiner and I was out to get it. He has committed many crimes known to the police'.

" 'I wasn't wearing a mask, that was a bandage. I've had bad headaches for a number of days. The wig and the false mustache were part of my disguise. I went into the captain's stateroom to arrest him'."

There was no doubt that the would-be pirate in his fright wig and low comedy false mustache was mentally addled, but Captain Reiner undoubtedly had a close call. Three years earlier another pair of outlaws, one of them also a former ship's officer, had boarded the Alaska Pacific Steamship Company's

HALF MILLION FEET OF LUMBER on the steam schooner *Davenport,* lower left, wouldn't make a dent in the forested shores of Puget Sound past which the little ship was steaming when this pre-World War I picture was taken.

PLOWING SOUTH AT EIGHT KNOTS, the little steam schooner *Whittier,* above, provided scant deck space for passengers and crew. Two of her seamen had evidently decided the only sitting space safe from slivvers was the main boom. Although the deck-loaded lumber carriers looked top-heavy and low in the water, ship's companys comforted themselves with the thought that the cargo was unsinkable.

An unusual deckload was being stowed aboard the Norwegian "turret-deck" steamship *Reidar* when the photograph at the left was taken in 1911, at Port Blakely. Unusual hull design made it possible to stow lumber alongside as well as in holds and on main deck.

Even big lumber carriers like the 5000-ton Hog-Islander *Liberty Glo* sometimes have deckload trouble. She's pictured below after returning to Port Angeles to restow a storm-battered cargo following a brush with a North Pacific gale about 1935.

SEAGOING LUMBER YARDS like these once carried Northwest forest products to California markets. Above, the skipper of the 456-ton *San Pedro* cons his ship from the flying bridge, that last slingload having blocked the view from the pilot house.

The *Oregon,* right, carried loads like this for Wilson Brothers, Grays Harbor lumbermen, until the depression of the 1930's put her out of work. The *Oregon,* with her fleet-mates *Idaho* and *Svea,* was scrapped in 1950.

The North Bend-built 750-ton *Fairhaven,* below, packed many loads like this between Puget Sound, Grays Harbor and San Francisco. In 1922 she tried a longer voyage to Mexico, and foundered at sea.

LUMBER FOR ALASKA is loaded aboard the Lowe Trading Company's *Redwood* at Seattle, circa 1935. This was one of the World War 1 wooden ships, some of which were converted to the steam schooner trade. The *Redwood* was launched at Bellingham in 1917.

coastwise liner *Buckman* as passengers. One of the two broke into Captain E. B. Wood's stateroom and killed him with a single blast of a sawed-off shotgun.

Captain Reiner's nerves were apparently unshaken, however, for he didn't stay in San Francisco even long enough for a soothing glass or two of steam beer. He took the *Willamette* butting out across the bar in the teeth of a storm that tore the San Francisco lightship loose from her moorings, capsized the steam schooner *Pomo* in Drake's Bay and had the *San Ramon, Daisy Putnam, Portland, Sue H. Elmore* and *Daisy Gadsby* bottled up at Astoria, unable to cross the Columbia River bar.

A little excitement was all in a day's work for a steam schooner skipper and the *Willamette,* like all ships of the well-run McCormick fleet, had a schedule to keep.

Captain Midnight Olsen of the steam schooner *Acme* was another skipper with a schedule to meet, for the *Acme* was more than just a lumber carrier. For many years she proudly flew a blue flag with *U.S. Mail* emblazoned on it in white letters. In addition to hauling lumber, general cargo and passengers between Humboldt Bay and San Francisco she also had the postal contract for that route. Captain Olsen took his postal duties seriously, determined that such things as storms and dark of night should not stay him on his appointed rounds.

He earned his nickname by often taking the little *Acme* careening across the Humboldt bar in the dark of night when things were kicking up to the point where his craft had twenty feet of water under her keel when she was on the crest of a wave and six inches when she was in the trough. Captain Mid-

PERT, PERKY and proudly flying Olson & Mahoney's houseflag, the steam schooner *Vanguard* churns up the Chehalis River past the Union Oil tanker *Whittier,* above. The *Pacific* (later *Barbara C.*), right, has just completed discharging her cargo at San Francisco; will soon be heading north for another load. *Tongass,* below, shown entering Seattle harbor from Alaska in 1946, is now moored at San Francisco under her original name, *Wapama*.

night took vast pride in the amazement of Eureka citizens when they woke up to find the bar breaking but the *Acme* safe at dock and the mail safe in their post office boxes.

Captain Olsen never lost a ship, but he did part with several thousand board feet of deck cargo during one particularly tumultuous crossing of the Humboldt bar, the lumber taking a fair share of the *Acme's* bulwarks along when it went overboard. When the battered steam schooner docked at San Francisco the skipper observed to his mate that their sailing schedule was still unbroken.

"Yah," the mate observed, "but ve boost up damn near everyt'ing else tryin' to do it."

This was the kind of straight-faced humor which gave the "Scandinavian Navy" a flavor all its own and has helped to make the memory of the steam schooners legendary along the coast from which they have long since vanished. Veterans of the lumber fleet still delight in recalling tales of Captain Hoodlum Bob Walvig of the *Cleone* and *Scotia,* who classed all argumentative deckhands as "hoodlums" and was known to take on three or four such at a time and "vip dem into shape" in short order; or of Safe-is-Open Gunderson, who scorned to trade punches with dissatisfied crew members. "Come to my room and I'll pay you off," Captain Gunderson would tell them. "The safe is always open." There was a Preacher John among the steam schooner captains, too, a pious soul who was, according to waterfront rumor, an ordained minister. His method

STEAM SCHOONER ALBUM

Left, top to bottom: *Oregon,* 989 tons, built by Andrew Peterson at Aberdeen in 1916, was operated by Wilson Brothers Lumber Co. until laid up on Oakland Creek about 1930. *Santiam,* 946 tons, built by John McDade at Fairhaven in 1916, was operated by Sudden & Christenson; burned at Aberdeen in 1936. *Santa Barbara* of J. R. Hanify fleet, 695 tons, built by W. G. Stone at San Francisco in 1900. Scrapped and hull placed in breakwater at San Francisco, 1943. *A. G. Lindsay,* built at Detroit, Michigan in 1889 for Great Lakes coal trade, was purchased in 1908 by a stock company headed by a Grays Harbor grocer. Intended for the coastal lumber trade, she ended up, after many financial reverses, as a fisheries tender in Alaska.

Above, top to bottom: *West Coast* loading on Lake Union, Seattle. *Newsboy* takes a sling-load of lumber in main hold. *Wellesley,* 700 tons, was built at Prosper, Oregon in 1907 by Heuckendorff; dismantled at Sausalito, 1943.

STEAM SCHOONER ALBUM

Above, top to bottom: *Helene,* 672 tons, built by Matthews at Hoquiam in 1906; foundered off the California coast, *Hollywood* was 250-foot World War I wooden ship built at Bellingham. *Tahoe,* 750 tons, built by Lindstrom at Hoquiam in 1907, was one of the unfortunate steam schooners which was assigned to hauling garbage for the city of Oakland; sold to South American owners in 1943.

Right, top to bottom: *Lassen,* 717 tons, built by Matthews at Hoquiam in 1917, was being used as a floating fish reduction plant when this picture was taken about 1938. She was broken up at Sausalito shortly thereafter. *Shna Yak,* 839 tons, built at Eagle Harbor in 1907, was renamed *Charles Christensen* in Sudden & Christenson service. Broken up at San Pablo, 1936. *Admiral Goodrich,* formerly the *Aroline* and later the *Noyo* (2) was in strange waters for a steam schooner when this picture was taken at Nome, Alaska in 1918. Later, as the *Noyo,* she was in the National Steamship Company's Mendocino Coast trade; stranded off Point Arena in 1932. *Wasp,* 641-tons, built by J. H. Price at Fairhaven in 1905 was operated for many years by Fred Linderman of San Francisco. She was destroyed by fire while under tow in Pensacola Bay, June, 1919.

AT THE HEAD OF NAVIGATION on Puget Sound, the 1200-ton steam schooner *Viking* was busily loading Douglas fir lumber from scows at the still uncompleted Port of Olympia dock when this photograph was taken in 1927. The *Viking,* built by the Rolph Shipbuilding Company at Rolph, California, in 1920, sank in Alaskan waters in 1943.

of dealing with ornery deckhands took the wind out of their sails as effectively as the ready fists of Hoodlum Bob. He would kneel on the deck and pray that heavenly guidance might change the ways of the erring seaman.

Of course the ships commanded by that seagoing sky-pilot were shunned by the old-timers who had learned their trade in the days of sail, for any real sailor knows that a preacher aboard ship is sure to bring bad luck.

Oliver Olson and Andy Mahoney were sensitive about this carry-over of windship superstitions to the steam schooner business, possibly because their company consisted of 13 stockholders, a number much dreaded by old shellbacks, who would rather jump ship than sail on a Friday the 13th. When the thirteenth ship to be added to their fleet, the *Rosalie Mahoney,* was taking shape on the ways of the Mathews Shipbuilding Company at Hoquiam, they decided to take drastic steps to bring enlightenment to the maritime world.

The *Rosalie Mahoney* (a thirteen-word name shared by Andy's wife and nine-year-old daughter who christened the ship) was launched on Friday, June 13, 1913. She slid down the ways at exactly 8:23 p.m. (the numbers add up to thirteen) flying thirteen signal flags. The thirteen members of the Olson and Mahoney families were present for the launching, which went off without a hitch.

Andy Mahoney had wanted to go all the way while they were at it and complete the defiance of superstition by breaking a mirror across the ship's nose at the launching instead of breaking a bottle of wine. But Olson, product of a long line of Norwegian seamen, balked at this.

"There might be something," he said thoughtfully, "in that mirror business."

Perhaps he was aware that the British Admiralty

had, many years earlier, sought to cast light on the darkness of seamen's superstitions by launching an H.M.S. *Friday* on a Friday the 13th and sending it off under the command of a Captain Friday for a 13-day shakedown cruise. H.M.S. *Friday* put out into the English Channel and has never been seen again to this day.

It was different with the *Rosalie Mahoney*. She led a particularly tranquil life in a dangerous trade. Her sister ships of the coastwise fleet capsized, piled up on the beach or rammed into each other, but the *Rosalie* just kept plugging up and down the coast hauling lumber until lumber was no longer shipped on wooden steam schooners. Then, with her name changed to *Border Queen,* she went to work hauling general freight between Seattle and British Columbia as one of the last active steam schooners on the coast.

Shortly after she was scrapped in the mid-1940's the *Seattle Times* published an interview with her builder G. F. Mathews, who was retired and living in Seattle.

"A lot of the old-timers watched the *Rosalie Mahoney* for a long time after she was placed in service, expecting her to burn up or go on the rocks," he recalled, "but she was luckier than most of the other steam schooners. She proved Andy Mahoney was right when he said there was nothing in that Friday the 13th foolishness."

Until the coming of highway and air transportation the most convenient and comfortable way of getting in and out of many smaller West Coast port towns was via steam schooner, many of which were fitted with passenger accommodations of varying degrees of comfort. Passengers who were in the know made their voyages on vessels of lines which made a sincere effort to treat their passengers well and maintain reasonable schedules. The McCormick schooners were particularly popular, for the company tried hard to make their passenger accommodations as nearly like those of the big steel coastal liners as the limited space aboard a wooden steam schooner would permit. Some of the larger ones even boasted miniature social halls and McCormick's *Celilo* enjoyed the crowning glory of an electric player-piano.

The unwary were sometimes lured aboard less desirable craft by hole-in-the-wall "travel agents," whose stock in trade was usually a large, framed lithograph of some three or four-funneled Atlantic ocean greyhound on the office wall. Assured by the wily agent that the ship he represented was "just about like that one there in the picture," the innocent traveler counted out his money and received a ticket good for "first class passage" to the port of his choice.

Much disillusioned after stumbling along some lumber-littered mill dock to discover that the fast and commodious S.S. *Maggie Murphy* was a battered wooden lumber drougher, the passenger was likely to find more frustrations on board. The craft might be commanded by one of the less progressive-minded of the Scandinavian Navy's officers who was stubbornly convinced that a steam schooner was designed for just one purpose; to carry lumber products. Not "svill." Certainly not ticket-holding landlubbers. Personality clashes were, under such circumstances, almost inevitable.

HEADED FOR ALASKA in Gold Rush days, the little 392-ton steam schooner *Arctic* had her long cargo booms stowed and everything else well lashed down in preparation for a long, rough trip. Many of the coastwise lumber carriers hauled passengers and freight north during the Klondike boom, but those that survived returned to more prosaic duties. The *Arctic,* built by Charles White at Bay City, Oregon in 1900, stranded off Point Arena with a redwood lumber cargo in 1922.

STEAM SCHOONER ALBUM

Left, top to bottom: *Aberdeen,* 500 tons, built by John Lindstrom at Aberdeen in 1899, struck the bar at San Francisco while serving as a garbage hauler in 1916, sinking with some loss of life. *Brookdale,* 2935-ton World War 1 ship, built at Aberdeen in 1918, converted to barge about 1940. *Fulton,* 380 tons, built by Bendixsen at Fairhaven in 1898. Operated in Seattle-Vancouver-Powell River general freight business by George Neimeyer from 1916 until taken over by Frank Waterhouse as first vessel of Borderline Transportation Co. Converted to floating cannery about 1928 and abandoned at Raymond, 1937. *Esther Johnson* was last wooden steam schooner built, launched at Portland in 1923.

Above, top to bottom: *Sierra,* 1286 tons and 225 feet long, was one of largest wooden steam schooners, built at North Bend in 1917 as the *Virginia Olson.* Served as Maritime Administration receiving ship at Seattle during World War 2 and still afloat in Lake Union, converted to diesel power. *Wilhelmina,* built along the lines of a miniature steam schooner, was powered by a heavy-duty gas engine; carried lumber and general cargo between Oregon coast secondary ports. *Brooklyn,* 334-ton single-ender built at Aberdeen by Lindstrom in 1901 foundered on the Humboldt bar in 1930.

STEAM SCHOONER ALBUM

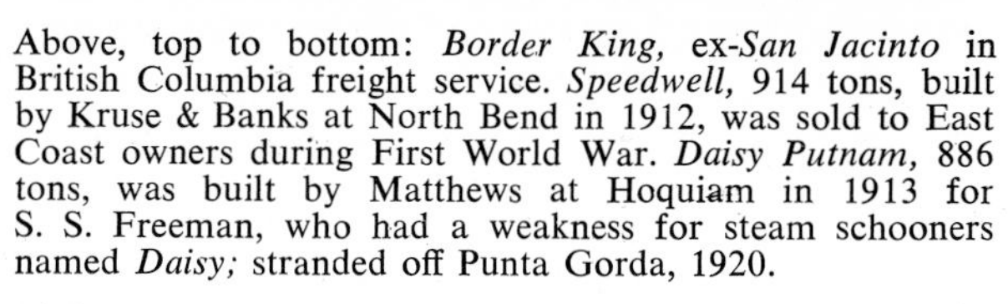

Above, top to bottom: *Border King,* ex-*San Jacinto* in British Columbia freight service. *Speedwell,* 914 tons, built by Kruse & Banks at North Bend in 1912, was sold to East Coast owners during First World War. *Daisy Putnam,* 886 tons, was built by Matthews at Hoquiam in 1913 for S. S. Freeman, who had a weakness for steam schooners named *Daisy;* stranded off Punta Gorda, 1920.

Right, top to bottom: *Bandon,* shown entering Eureka harbor about 1940, was beached at Bandon, Oregon a few months later. She was built at North Bend in 1907. *Fort Bragg* is shown here towing the capsized *Wasp* into San Francisco Bay. Only the keel of the *Wasp* is visible alongside the *Fort Bragg,* but she was salvaged and put back in service. The *Fort Bragg,* built by Price at Fairhaven in 1900, was a 700-tonner operated by Charles H. Higgins. She stranded at Coos Bay in 1932. *Willapa* (2) was later renamed *Florence Olson;* foundered off Port Orford, 1941. *Thomas L. Wand,* 657 tons, Aberdeen-built by Lindstrom in 1906, stranded at Point Sur, 1933.

STOWING REDWOOD AT FORT BRAGG, the little *Coquille River,* built at Prosper, Oregon in 1896, was the pride and joy of Captain "Saturday-Night" Jack Bostrom, who always tried to have his steam schooner alongside the mill dock in time for the Saturday night country dance at the Fort Bragg schoolhouse.

The *Tongass,* below, looked sad and forlorn with her nose in the weeds at the St. Vincent de Paul dock in Seattle, but now she's spruce and chipper again, restored to her old name, *Wapama* by the California State Park Commission.

If the misguided passenger happened to have his bride along, having contemplated his voyage as an idyllic honeymoon cruise, there was the possibility of further complications. The minute "staterooms" aboard most steam schooners were fitted with three shelflike bunks and, if trade was brisk, the rascally ticket agent had probably sold the "Aunt Mary," as the top bunk was called in steam schooner parlance, to some perfect stranger.

Back in the spring of 1911 the writer's grandparents, Dr. and Mrs. E. C. Story took the sternwheel steamboat *Harbor Belle* down the Chehalis River from their home at Montesano to board the steam schooner *Coronado* at Aberdeen. Their luggage included tents, bedsprings and cooking equipment, for they proposed to camp on the beach at Long Beach and later attend the Festival of Flowers at Los Angeles, where President Teddy Roosevelt would lead a troop of Roughriders in the parade. The journal of that trip indicates some of the informalities of travel aboard even such a respectable steam schooner as the *Coronado:*

HEFTY HULL LINES of later-day steam schooner is displayed by *Cornelia* of Kitsap Lumber Company in drydock at Seattle, 1937. A ship of many names, she was launched at Oakland in 1917 as the *Robert C. Sudden,* served during first world war as French S.S. *Hadrumete,* returned to Sudden & Christensen operation under her original name, later rechristened *John C. Kirkpatrick.*

Reminders of wooden lumber ship era are the three-masted schooner *Wawona* and the former steam schooner *Sierra* (ex-*Virginia Olson*) now converted to a motorship, both presently moored in Lake Union at Seattle.

March 18:

Left Montesano at noon today and was met with delay and disappointment at the outset, the boat being one hour late on account of the funeral of Mr. Tom Morgan's little boy—and two hours and a half late starting back waiting for the people to come from the grave, but as usual all things come to an end and at last we started and in due time reached Aberdeen and was put aboard the steamer Coronado *which by the way is a fine boat with all the staterooms etc. amidship, which makes her ride very nicely. As she was billed to leave on Thursday at 3 a.m. we were obliged to go home with Jim who was down to the ship to see us off. So up town we trudged and after supper back we trudged and in due time tucked ourselves in our little bunks.*

March 19:

The boat left the wharf on time and when we got up this morning we were on the broad ocean, but unless you looked upon its vastness you would not have believed it. A mill pond couldn't be smoother.

LOADING GENERAL CARGO FOR ALASKA, the *Evelyn Berg* found a new job with the Alaska Transportation Company during the lean years of the 1930's. Built at Everett in 1905 as the *Johan Poulson,* this old-timer sank in northern waters in 1938.

The *Hornet,* lower left, was a sturdy unit of Fred Linderman's legendary "Insect Line." This 697-ton, 176-foot "stem-winder" was built at Aberdeen in 1906.

HEADED FOR THE MILL DOCK, the steam schooner *Phyllis* plows up Willapa Bay, booms rigged and ready to start loading in the 1928-vintage photograph above. Built at Aberdeen in 1917, the *Phyllis* stranded off Port Orford in 1935. *Anne Hanify,* pictured at the right as a brand-new unit of the J. R. Hanify Lumber Company fleet in 1920, ended her days in a blaze of glory off Grays Harbor in 1949 as the Mexican S. S. *Salina Cruz. Brunswick,* below, lived to a ripe old age. Built at North Bend in 1898, this diminutive 500-tonner survived until post-World War 2 days.

At dinner our ill luck came up when the captain informed me, in answer to my question of when we would reach San Pedro, that they would stop at Redondo two or three days to discharge the most of their cargo and that the passengers were expected to leave there and on looking at our tickets found they were only for Redondo, so what we are going to do is still a mystery. The sea has been as smooth as a floor all day, but as the berths are so very narrow the Dr. didn't rest well at all.

March 20:

Today has been just as smooth as yesterday. Mattie was some sea sick, but the others of us were all O.K. We spent most of the day on the hurricane deck or, as small boy on board called it, the roof. Saw a number of whales, porpoises, etc.

March 21:

Today has been as like yesterday as two peas in a pod. We have gotten quite well acquainted with most of the passengers, but as there were none especially nice there is no need to mention them.

March 22:

This morning we were at the wharf in San Francisco and as we were to be there until 10 a.m. after breakfast we took a car and went to the Golden Gate Park. We got back to the steamer in good time, but were kept from starting by some of the other passengers being late, but at last we were off. The poor captain was wild with the delay and after we started he found that the 2nd mate was drunk, but after he had relieved his feelings by helping (?) the drunken mate to his room and cussing a little to the crew he cooled down and all went well. We took on a number of new passengers at the city, one of whom loaned me the Call *and I read the first part of a new story.*

March 24:

The only thing wherein yesterday was unlike the other days was in my reading the hands of most of the officers and passengers. This morning we were off from Redondo when we awoke and after breakfast we went up to the wharf where all the passengers got off and we were obliged to do the same as Capt. Petersen said it was against the rules to allow anyone but those working to stay on board while unloading, but that the Centralia *was going to start for San Pedro about ten and as the same company owned both boats we could go in her, but we couldn't take our baggage as there was no way for a team to get from one wharf to the other. So as the ill luck still stuck by us we started for the* Centralia *in a nice little Washington rain, but as I was used to that I went on the beach and picked up some lovely mosses and one agate. After we had been on the* Centralia *for a while, but before she left, Capt. P. came over from the* Coronado *and said he had found a way to get our things over on a truck on the railroad and in a few moments they came. We left the wharf at about 11:30 and reached San P. about two thirty, but it was so changed we hardly knew it and could see no place to tent.*

Grandmother, who was as superstitious as any steam schooner skipper, persisted in attributing all the frustrations of the voyage to the fact that "meeting a funeral was bad luck" and vowed that if it ever happened again she would "go back and make a new beginning." In due time, however, a suitable "tenting" spot was found, excellent beach combing for shells, agates and beach mosses was indulged in and Teddy Roosevelt was seen at first hand gracing the *Fiesta de la Flores* astride his white charger. On May 29 the return voyage to Grays Harbor began, once more aboard the *Coronado,* but not until Grandmother had visited a professional palmist in Los Angeles, who assured her that all would be well on the return trip.

May 29:

Mathea got us up a little after five and as soon as breakfast was over we pulled down the tents and by 11 we were all ready. After dinner the team came and in a short time it was loaded. The Coronado *had gone over to the other side so all of our things had to be loaded in a small boat and taken across. In getting them on the ship they dropped one of our trunks in the salt water. When we got on board we opened it and took the wet things out to dry. At 6:30 we cast off. About 7:30 it began to get foggy and now the fog horn is blowing regularly.*

May 30:

The fog held all day and it was so cold and disagreeable we all spent the greater part of the day in our berths to keep warm. It was as if nature was in sympathy with the day.

May 31:

We reached San Francisco about 12:30 and visited ashore until half past five when we returned to the ship and found it deserted by all save the passengers and no supper. So we began a skirmish around to find something. I got some crackers and butter, a piece of cold meat and some lukewarm coffee. After a while we found the raw materials for a regular meal and after 8 o'clock we had supper. The M.D. (Grandfather) and one of the other passengers, a young man, went down to the galley and cooked it and we set the table and found the things upstairs. We had beefsteak and bacon, canned corn, plums, soup, coffee and bread and butter. I tell you it was

EARLY DOUBLE-ENDER of the West Coast steam schooner fleet was the *Rainier*, pictured here leaving Grays Harbor with a full cargo of Douglas fir lumber. Passengers favored the amidships accommodations which eliminated some of the vibration and motion of the earlier "stem-winders."

good. We left all the dirty dishes and I expect the air will be blue in the morning.

June 1:

I was a good prophet. The air was blue and the clouds lowered for some time, but cleared in time and we got something to eat this morning. The wind blew quite hard yesterday, but this morning it was a gale. After dinner the steamer changed wharves and took on a lot of new passengers and much freight. We were to go out at one o'clock p.m., but as the wind still blew a gale it was deemed best to wait until morning so if nothing new arises we start at 4 a.m. We made up a party of ourselves and a young man who we have nicknamed "My Son" as his old mother is with him and that is what she calls him, and went uptown to the Alcazar Theater and saw the play of "The Tyranny of Tears." It was very good, but upset the old idea that tears are a woman's last and best weapon.

June 2:

At 4:30 a.m. we left the wharf. The wind was still blowing, but the ocean was much calmer than we had feared it would be. Still the waves had power to toss the ship in pretty good shape and the sea itself was a very pretty sight as the sun was shining bright, which made the water bright sparkling blue and the wind was strong enough to toss it into great waves capped with white and as they would break catch the spray and cast it high in the air. About supper time the wind went down considerably and the evening was fine, the young moon lighting up the dark waters and the ship rolls just enough to be pleasant.

Grandmother's personal log ends at this point. Whether the remainder of the voyage to Grays Harbor was too uneventful to merit recording, or whether things got worse and she became too seasick to write, remains lost to history.

END OF THE LINE for many of the wooden lumber carriers came with the world-wide depression of the 1930's. Some survived as barges, like those pictured above at Eagle Harbor, Washington. Others, like the little Wilson Brothers steam schooner *Svea,* below, ended their days on "Rotten Row," where they fell apart in the mudflats or were demolished by junkies in search of scrap metal.

What she did write is now a chapter out of the half-forgotten past. Although the little wooden steam schooners survived in some numbers until the depression years of the 1930's, the coast guard and steamboat inspectors took a dim view of their fitness as passenger carriers. Cargos of seasoned lumber stowed on wooden ships with oil-soaked bilges presented an undeniable hazard, although surprisingly few of them were actually destroyed by fire.

None of them were blessed with such refinements as watertight doors and as they aged the wooden hulls became anything but leak-proof. Not overpowered in their prime, they became slower than ever and suffered frequent mechanical breakdowns at sea, yet they continued to nose in and out of sketchy "ports" that other sea-going ships avoided like the plague. Along the way they usually ambled along within sight of the breaker line, which simplified navigation but left scant sea room in case of emergency.

The steam schooners were an integral part of the glory days of logging and sawmilling on America's last frontier. They were a rugged and unique breed, those West Coast steam schooners, as were the timber beasts ashore, who carried their blanket-rolls from camp to camp, and the men like Captain Rainwater Oscar Johnson and Hands and Feet Hansen and Scantling Bill Roberts and Yib-boom Yohnson who sailed those ships of the "Scandinavian Navy" from San Pedro to Puget Sound.

Chapter 3

MILL PORTS

Ship on Hall Shipyard ways, Port Blakely.

HENRY YESLER brought the first steam sawmill to the Puget Sound country and set it up on the waterfront of the infant village named Seattle, after the kindly and dignified Indian who was chief of the Duwamish and Suquamish tribes. Yesler's mill never got very big or made him very much money, but it gave Seattle its first industry and its start toward becoming one of America's great cities.

Across the Sound the great mills at the sawdust towns of Port Ludlow, Port Gamble, Port Madison, Port Blakely, Port Discovery, Utsalady and Seabeck reversed that trend, earning huge fortunes for their owners and, in the end, leaving only deserted villages. Some of the once roaring mill ports of Puget Sound have, indeed, vanished almost completely. Separated from the rest of the nation by miles of deep salt water, their reason for existence vanished with the great forests that once surrounded them.

With logging and sawmilling entering the realm of "big business," the 1880's are recalled by old-timers as the great days of the industry in the Pacific Northwest. There was almost no government interference and taxes, by present-day standards, were negligible. It was generally assumed that the region's forest resources were inexhaustible. Only prime trees were cut, with ten or twelve feet at the base left as stumps and the tops, from the first branches upward burned in "slashing fires" which sometimes got out of control to consume thousands of acres of virgin timber. During the summer months the skies were usually hidden behind the pall of burning forests.

In mid-September of 1902 Seattle papers devoted their entire front pages to accounts of the ravages of forest fires. On September 12 the *Times* reported:

"Dense clouds of smoke overhang the entire western slope of Washington and Oregon, from the Cascades to the sea. Forest fires without number are burning fiercely in the mountains and foothills and a hundred villages and towns are threatened with total destruction. Seattle is almost cut off from telegraphic and telephone communication with the outside world. The situation is the worst in the history of the great Pacific Northwest. Hundreds of lives may have been sacrificed to the greed of the fire demon.

"At Portland and Tacoma black clouds of smoke obscure the sun and both cities are in almost total darkness. Olympia is badly off. In Seattle at high noon the light was little better than that which prevails an hour after sunset. Lights were burned in all the stores and in many offices. By 4 o'clock lights were universally in use throughout the city.

"Mariners on Puget Sound are faring badly. The Sound is overhung with smoke and many of the steamers are forced to run at half speed. Landmarks by the aid of which captains guide their vessels are entirely hidden by the universal smoke."

The Seventh Day Adventists, holding a large camp meeting near Olympia, proclaimed that the universal darkness was proof that the world was about to come to an end, but the papers reported, "As a rule, laughter and fun prevail."

Mill hands worked hard from six in the morning until six at night for a dollar a day plus room and board and on payday the company got most of its cash outlay back at the company store or saloon.

Cyrus Walker, who headed the Pope and Talbot timber empire of four big mills in three mill towns, opposed heavy drinking and loose women, probably less on moral grounds than on the theory that a mill hand who has been out raising hell all night is in no shape to begin an honest day's work at six o'clock in the morning. Women of easy virtue, as they were called in Victorian days, were not permitted to ply their profession in the Pope and Talbot mill towns of Port Gamble, Port Ludlow and Utsalady, but colonies of beach shacks with red lanterns in the windows sprang up conveniently nearby. At Port Gamble a regular fleet of rowboats plied between the waterfront and "Little Boston" across the bay, filled with loggers, millhands and sailors.

Liquor was sold at the company store, but the heavy drinking and high-stakes poker games at the privately-owned Puget Hotel in Port Gamble were too rich for Cyrus Walker's taste. He finally had to buy the hotel and place it under company management.

Walker's Port Gamble house was destroyed by fire in 1885 and he decided to move his capitol to Port Ludlow. The Ludlow Mill, the one that W. F. Sayward had been building when Captain Talbot explored the Sound in 1853, had been purchased by Pope and Talbot in 1879, but the lumber market was somewhat depressed and the company was busy modernizing the old Cranney and Grannon mill at Utsalady on Camano Island. This plant, which produced the finest ship's spars in the world, had been taken over in 1877.

As a result, Port Ludlow was in the doldrums for several years. In 1881 shipbuilder Henry Hall described it as follows:

"This town consists of a store; a saw-mill which has been 4 years in building and has not been started yet; a hotel, the Phoenix, of which I am the only guest, and which only lodges its guests; a cook house, run by a Chinaman, at which meals are obtained; a few cabins for workmen in the shipyard; two or three houses; and the shipyard. A lonely place."

The Hall Brothers, of which Henry was a member, had already moved their shipyard operations to Port Blakely, after having built 31 fine lumber ships at Ludlow, but all this was changed two years later. The mill was turning out 100,000 feet of lumber daily and the old Hall shipyard was being operated by Pope and Talbot. All the mills closed down on July 22, 1884 and the employees from Utsalady and Port Gamble were taken to Port Ludlow on the company's side-wheel mill tugs to celebrate the launching of the 140-foot propeller tug *Tyee*.

Real splendor came to Port Ludlow when Cyrus Walker moved to town in 1885. His house, Admiralty Hall, was finished in 1887, built of the choicest lumber that the Pope and Talbot mills could produce. The spacious interior, finished in grained Douglas fir, was filled with ponderous black walnut furniture and antiques brought around Cape Horn by sailing ship.

Admiralty Hall dominated the town from a rolling slope which furnished a heady view of Ludlow

Bay and Admiralty Inlet. The front lawn boasted a cannon which fired salutes to favored ships when they entered the bay and at the sides and back were formal gardens and a private menagerie of native wild animals.

Frugal Yankee though he was, Cyrus Walker entertained lavishly at Admiralty Hall, even compromising his scruples by maintaining a fine wine cellar and ample liquor cabinet for the refreshment of guests who were in a position to do something profitable in return for Pope and Talbot.

Since most of the Northwest lumbermen came originally from Maine, the mill towns were often replicas of neat New England villages. In Port Gamble the company even built a church which is an almost exact duplicate of the Congregational Church at East Machias, Maine. The original Maine families formed the aristocracy of the mill towns. One tale is told of an unfortunate fellow who fell off the mill dock at Port Gamble. No attention was

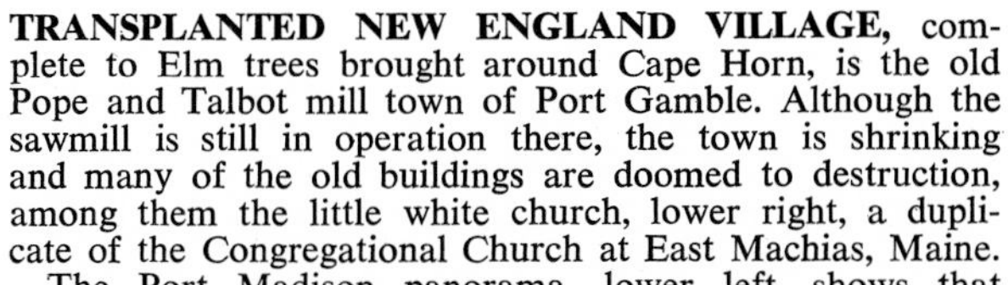
TRANSPLANTED NEW ENGLAND VILLAGE, complete to Elm trees brought around Cape Horn, is the old Pope and Talbot mill town of Port Gamble. Although the sawmill is still in operation there, the town is shrinking and many of the old buildings are doomed to destruction, among them the little white church, lower right, a duplicate of the Congregational Church at East Machias, Maine.
The Port Madison panorama, lower left, shows that booming mill town in the 1880's when Meig's mill was working from dawn to dark to fill the holds of waiting ships.

PORT GAMBLE BAY WAS THRONGED WITH SHIPS a half century ago and the steam tug *Pioneer* had her hands full guiding big square-riggers like those pictured above to proper moorages while they waited their turn at the mill dock.

paid to him as he alternately gasped for air and shouted for help. As he came up from the depths for the third time a man on the dock glanced down at him casually; then shouted, "Blow the whistle and call the mill crew! *He's* from East Machias!"

These were the days when the tidewater sawmills echoed to the scream of the head-saws and a vast fleet of ships gorged on the lumber on the mill docks until their holds were full and the deckloads rose ten feet above their bulwarks. Another fleet of mill tugs strained against the tides of Puget Sound as they hauled long booms of logs to feed the saws. The mill town harbors were often paved solidly for half their width with logs, leaving scant room for the row upon row of sailing ships which waited for loading space at the dock.

Some of the world's most beautiful ships were to be found thus tied to log booms in the Northwest mill ports. The *Palmyra* and *Carondelet* sailed regularly out of Port Gamble. The last of the Donald McKay clippers, *Glory of the Seas,* hauled lumber from Puget Sound in her old age, and even the lovely British tea clipper *Thermopylae,* to whom a rival captain once signaled, "Goodby! You are too much for us—you are the finest model of a ship I ever saw—it does my heart good to look at you."

At the turn of the century a working agreement was made between Western railroads and millmen which made rail shipment of timber products economically feasible, a factor which was not healthy for the lumber ships or the mill ports. Between 1897 and 1904 the amount of lumber shipped from the

EMPTY BAY AND NEGLECTED CEMETERY bear mute witness to Port Gamble's decline. Fenced in plot is grave of an army private killed in the Indian War of 1856. The Puget Hotel, lower right, remains in operation, as does the sawmill in the background, but most millworkers commute to the job by automobile and mill's cut is shipped by scow.

Next page: Ships at the mill dock, Port Blakely, about 1910.

"LIVELIEST PLACE ON PUGET SOUND" in 1866 was the Hood Canal mill town of Seabeck, pictured here in that era. The side-wheel tug *Colfax,* one of the first on Puget Sound. lay at the mill dock, ready to haul logs or sailing ships. The big sawmill, built by Marshal Blinn, was destroyed by fire in the mid-1880's; Seabeck is a sleepy village now, its only "industry" a large conference grounds and camp maintained by a religious group.

Puget Sound area increased six hundred per cent. By 1906 rail shipments exceeded water-borne cargos by four hundred million feet.

The St. Paul & Tacoma Lumber Company mills at Tacoma, designed to manufacture lumber for the "rail trade," were outproducing the Port Blakely Mill Company's giant plant, which had been acclaimed as the biggest sawmill in the world under one roof. Even the Grays Harbor Commercial Company's huge Cosmopolis mill, producer of more lumber than any other mill on Grays Harbor, was shipping 33 million feet of its 39 million-foot annual cut by rail.

Of course the coastwise lumber trade still relied heavily on ships, as did the overseas markets across the Pacific, but the mill ports, separated from the nearest railways by miles of deep water, were at a decided disadvantage. Marshall Blinn's mill at Seabeck, which had been producing a hundred thousand feet of lumber a day, was totally destroyed by fire in 1886 and was not rebuilt. The Utsalady mill closed during the hard times of the early 1890's and never reopened.

The sawmill business reached its peak in 1909 with a cut of more than 45 billion feet, after which the demand for lumber as a building commodity began its long decline. There were other factors at work, too. The government began to view its remaining forest lands as a national asset to be maintained for the benefit of all its citizens rather than something to be scalped for the enrichment of a few. Public opinion changed toward the lumbermen too. Once regarded as economic pioneers, they were, in the words of Stewart Holbrook, "Surprised one day to find themselves public ogres who fairly sweated destruction from every pore and ate up everything but the sawdust, which they left in unslightly piles. The timber baron became a notable figure in the American demonology, complete with peaveys for horns, and the tail a long, curling ribbon of bandsaw."

A new generation of lumbermen now views

A MILL PORT IS WHERE THE TREES ARE. This floating donkey engine hauled felled timber to salt water at Arcadia, on upper Puget Sound, at the turn of the century.

Northwest timber as a crop, to be harvested carefully and painstakingly replanted. Not even the sawdust is wasted now, being compressed into cylinders as fireplace fuel. As a result of the view that the forests are not inexhaustible they may, in fact, become so. There are still big mills in business and some of them even continue to ship part of their output by sea, in the holds and on the decks of big seagoing steel freighters, but only one of the legendary mill ports remains active, and that on a limited scale.

The Port Ludlow mill shut down during the depression of the 1930's. Cyrus Walker's stately Admiralty Hall was torn down in 1937. Today only the concrete remains of the boiler room and a few rotten pilings show where the giant mill and ship-lined dock once stood.

Pope and Talbot Inc. still operates its Port Gamble mill, but with only half as many men as were employed there at the peak of its production. The town itself is shrinking, too, for the company-owned town is a thing of the past. Workers prefer to commute to work by automobile from their own homes. Eventually the company plans to compress its replica of a Maine seaport town into a single block of homes maintained for mill officials. The general store, where buttonhooks, horse collars and corsets are still on display, will be retained, as will the ornate Puget Hotel, but the white clapboard church, patterned after the one in East Machias, is slated for destruction.

Most of the mill's output is moved by barge to railway yards or piers in Seattle and the lumber ships are long gone from Gamble Bay. Port Gamble, like Port Townsend, has something of an air of unreality about it. There is the feeling that time has stood still there and the expectation that a blast of Cyrus Walker's cannon may yet salute the arrival of some stately square-rigger that, like Pope and Talbot's mill town, has lost its way in time and space.

Port Blakely shipyard, above. Lumber ships waiting loading space at mill dock in the background.

Company houses at Port Blakely, mill dock in the background, below.

Stern-loading of long timbers, Port Blakely, above.

"Biggest sawmill in the world" at Port Blakely, log storage grounds in foreground, below.

LUMBER SCHOONER LAUNCHING AT HALL'S PORT BLAKELY SHIPYARD was always a gala occasion. School was dismissed and steamboats usually brought crowds across the Sound from Seattle to see the big event. Henry K. Hall, operator of the mill town shipyard, is the bearded gentleman in the center foreground.

CYRUS WALKER, emperor of the Pope and Talbot Northwest sawmill empire, used the little steam launch *Hyak,* above, to cruise between company towns and take guests on salmon fishing excursions. But when he wasn't using her for such pleasant purposes, the *Hyak* had to work hard at juggling logs in the Port Gamble booming grounds.

Much of the furniture in the Puget Hotel, colorful Port Gamble landmark of today, was brought around Cape Horn by 19th century sailing ships, left.

The Port Gamble street below is lined with houses once occupied by mill officials. The less pretentious homes of the millworkers were on the other side of town, separated from "boss's row" by the high ground of the town cemetery.

GIANT LOG RAFTS like the one pictured on the opposite page, top, and the one below being moved down the Columbia River by the stern-wheel towboats *Hercules* and *Cascades,* once challenged steam schooners as means of hauling lumber coastwise to California. The big tug *Roosevelt,* formerly Admiral Peary's polar exploration ship, specialized in such coastwise log towing. Modern lograft transportation is illustrated at left, opposite page, as a powerful diesel tug of the Canadian Kingcome Navigation moves a Davis raft from northern British Columbia logging camp to a Powell River Forest Products Company mill.

MARI

Square-rigger crossing the Columbia River bar.

Next page: American bark *Burgess* towing into Puget Sound in ballast.

TRIM FOUR-MASTED SCHOONER *Lottie Bennett,* Page 127, was launched at the Hall Shipyard, Port Blakely, in 1899. Like most of the tall-masted Hall schooners, she was a fast and handy sailer; was photographed at Seattle in 1915 after having entered port under her own power.

WINDSHIP DETAILS: The wheel and binnacle of the lumber schooner *Commodore* were photographed, above, as she lay at anchor in Eagle Harbor in 1935.

Her jutting bowsprit, with headsails furled, made a salty perch for a visiting Puget Sound seagull, below.

WATERLOGGED AND WALLOWING, the schooner *Alice Cooke,* Port Blakely-built by Hall in 1891, found temporary shelter in that handy refuge for storm-battered ships, Neah Bay, seven miles inside the grim headland of Cape Flattery. She was one of a dozen lumber schooners to meet trouble off the Cape in a series of December storms in 1909. Unlike most of them, *Alice Cooke* managed to hang on to her deckload.

Opposite page: Tall masts of the schooner *Commodore*.

Lumber schooners *Mary E. Foster* and *Bainbridge* in the Strait of Juan de Fuca.

SHIP'S CAT has proverbial easy life aboard the *Conqueror*, last of the West Coast barkentines.

Schooner *Vigilant*

RACING SCHOONER HIGH AND DRY. Five-masted schooner *Vigilant,* legendary rival of the *Commodore* on the Honolulu run in the 1930's, goes on the Eagle Harbor drydock for an overhaul.

LOADING LUMBER AT OLYMPIA, the barkentine *Conqueror* was photographed by the writer with his trusty Brownie camera in 1927 as she prepared for her last voyage, opposite page, left. The years had dealt roughly with her when the Williamson photo, opposite page, bottom, was taken on August 30, 1943, shortly before she was burned for scrap.

A typical square-rigger crew was that of the down-easter *Santa Clara,* Bath-built in 1879, photographed at San Francisco in 1916. Her skipper, Captain J. Bertonccini, is in the front row in shore-going clothes.

Splicing an eye in a manila line, the two seamen, below, helped sail the barkentine *Conqueror* on her last voyage under sail . . . from Puget Sound to South Africa and back in 1927-28.

CAPTAIN B. N. A. (NELS) KRANTZ, above, was one of the last of the lumber schooner masters. From 1919 to 1923 he sailed on the *Alice Cooke* as first mate with Captain William Burmeister. When Captain Burmeister took command of the *Commodore,* Krantz went with him as mate, taking over as skipper from 1929 until 1935 when the *Commodore* was sold.

Captain Krantz and the *Commodore* figured in a legendary sailing ship race during the winter of 1931-32. The *Commodore* left Honolulu in ballast for Puget Sound on November 20; the five-masted *Vigilant,* Captain Mellberg, followed on November 26. Thirty-one days later the *Commodore* was taken in tow by the tug *Goliath* off Cape Flattery, but the hawser broke in gale-swept seas off the Cape. The schooner drifted 200 miles up the Vancouver Island coast, fighting 90-mile winds. Meanwhile the *Vigilant* made it in to the shelter of the Strait, 39 days and one hour out of Honolulu. Old sailors still argue over who won the race. On a "tug-to-tug" basis the *Commodore* won, but on an "into-the-Strait" basis it was the *Vigilant.*

Captain Krantz died in the autumn of 1959 at the age of 81.

REMINDER OF THINGS PAST. The three-masted wooden schooner *C. A. Thayer,* built at Fairhaven, California in 1895, was rescued from an Olympic Peninsula beach in 1957 and refitted at Seattle for permanent moorage as a unit of San Francisco's marine museum fleet. The pictures on these pages were taken just before her departure from Seattle for a final voyage under sail to San Francisco. Above she's moored at a Port of Seattle pier awaiting drydocking, the river stern-wheeler *Skagit Belle* in the background. Pictured below is the crew that sailed her to San Francisco, headed by Captain A. F. Raynaud, veteran sailing ship master.

OUTWARD-BOUND FROM SEATTLE for a permanent home in San Francisco, the *C. A. Thayer* is towed toward Cape Flattery by a Puget Sound tug, above.

The handsome *Inca,* left, was the first of the five-masted schooners built by Hall's Port Blakely shipyard. She was launched in 1896.

SCHOONER SOPHIE CHRISTENSEN, shown loading at Puget Sound mill dock, above, was later operated in Bering Sea fishery trade by Captain J. E. Shields of Seattle, who gained fame in private war against Japanese fish poachers in Alaska waters before World War 2.

JAPANESE SQUARES, rough timbers for shipment to Japanese finishing mills, are moved toward a trans-Pacific freighter in Tacoma harbor by Olson Tugboat Company's small but husky *Paddy Craig,* right.

Chapter 4

OUTPORTS AND DOG HOLES

MOST people were preoccupied with gold in the San Francisco of 1850, but Harry Meiggs, promoter, engineer and practitioner of frenzied finance, was not entirely blinded by the glittering stuff that was coming down the Sacramento River from the diggings. He cast a canny eye on a new product that was being shipped down from the Mendocino coast and piled in handsome dark-red stacks on his North Beach wharf. It was redwood lumber and disillusioned miners who had wandered back to San Francisco from the north claimed the forests up that way had no end; that even a middle-sized redwood tree had enough lumber in it to build a half dozen churches.

Meiggs decided that the big trees would be a lot easier to find than gold and would probably be making money for somebody long after the richest mining claim had petered out. Being a persuasive man, he had no difficulty in convincing others that a modern sawmill on the California redwood coast would be a profitable venture. Among his associates was Edward C. Williams, who owned a lumber yard and was selling all the redwood lumber he could get his hands on.

Meiggs had looked over a little circular sawmill at Bodega, but it could only turn out eight thousand feet of lumber in a twelve-hour day. Such a small time operator didn't interest Meiggs, who observed with scorn that a carpenter could carry the planks away and nail them up faster than a mill like that could turn them out. He bought the mill anyway, since it was the best available, but dispatched young Williams to the East Coast to superintend the building of the machinery for a modern gang mill.

Upon the arrival of the mill machinery by sailing ship around Cape Horn, Meiggs bought the ship *Ontario,* loaded his equipment aboard, hired a crew of carpenters and set out for Big River, 120 miles to the north.

The indefatigable Mr. Williams had already explored the timberlands in that area and sent back a glowing report. Meiggs made the voyage north on the *Ontario*. The trip was blessed with unusually fine weather, which was a blessing. The ship had been abandoned by her crew in 1849 and had been at anchor for so long that her planks above the waterline had shrunk and let most of the oakum fall out of the seams. As a result she leaked like a basket, even though the sea was mild. The carpenters and laborers had to be put on the payroll and used to pump ship, but the *Ontario* finally wallowed up to her landfall off Big River and worked her way into the modest cove which was the nearest thing to a harbor in that vicinity.

Williams' report on the timber potential hadn't been exaggerated. The giant redwoods cast their shadows on the waters of the cove and marched inland for miles. Meiggs established his mill near the settlement of Big River, later known at Mendocino City. He ran the decrepit *Ontario* ashore and had her holds filled with rocks, the idea being that she would form the nucleus of a permanent breakwater and wharf for the loading of lumber schooners.

Meiggs hadn't counted on the violence with which the Pacific Ocean can hammer the sketchy "harbors" of the redwood coast. The first full-scale winter storm tore the poor old *Ontario* limb from limb and strewed the pieces for miles along the coast.

DOWN TO THE SEA ON A WIRE, redwood lumber is stacked high on all the usable deck space of the 123-foot *Gualala,* above, in a typical Mendocino Coast dog hole loading operation.

The loggers and millmen who followed Meiggs in staking claims along the timber-clad gulches of the Mendocino coast soon conceded that conventional loading methods just wouldn't work for them. They abandoned the idea of building docks and contrived a shakily awe-inspiring device called the apron chute.

The Stewart & Hunter operation at Newport was typical and is described by Ralph W. Andrews in his book *Redwood Classic:*

"The lumber was hauled by six-horse teams and hand-made wagons from the mill to the shipping point and piled at the chute head, seventy feet above the pounding surf.

"This chute extended some eighty feet down and out over the rocks, the whole spidery contraption supported by a trestle and a type of A-frame. The apron or thirty-foot extreme lower section was suspended by a cable from the A-frame and swayed in the perpetual wind like a grasshopper's antenae.

"When one of the little single-ender lumber schooners was ready to chance an entrance to the channel between the rocks, she would signal ashore and prepare for the ordeal. This might take a few hours or a few days, depending on the weather and tide. Even after anchoring a ship might have to pull up and run for it, the loading operation halted until she got back into the dog hole again.

"This anchoring process was at once an art, a specialized skill attempted only by the brave or the simple-minded. Having no shelter from the merciless wind and wild breakers, the shoals shallow and treacherous, a skipper would lay-to as close to the jagged rocks as possible and at just the right opportunity order full steam ahead. He had only one chance. If he missed it, the ship was aground and already being battered to pieces. Once into the hole, anchors would be dropped fore and aft and the ship winched either way to settle her as near the bottom end of the chute as possible. Sometimes spring lines were used to allow for a twenty-five foot rise and fall of the ocean swells under the chute.

"High above the schooner's deck, riding the swaying apron was the clapperman, more catty and contemptuous of danger than any steel-rigger on solid footing. At his signal the feeder sent boards rattling down the greased chute until it was full. Then, if the

DOGHOLE DROUGHERS OF THE REDWOOD COAST, steam schooners *Pomo, Gualala* and *Pasadena* loading in the doubtful shelter of Albion Harbor, where a water-powered mill was first operated in 1853. The *Pasadena* was the first steam schooner to use oil as fuel, but back in 1893 this was considered such a dangerous innovation that San Francisco port authorities refused to allow her to dock there and she had to go back to coal.

ship was under him, he would release the first piece of lumber by dropping the hinged 'apron' at the chute end, the gap filling up from above. Then another and another as long as he had a deck to drop to. And so, in two or three days if all went well, the load was made up—seventy five to one hundred thousand feet of redwood ties, shingles, fence posts or timbers on their uncertain way to market."

The devious financial schemes of Harry Meiggs soon made it advisable for him to skip town, leaving an outraged throng of bankers, money-lenders and assorted creditors in his wake, but the mill he built at Mendocino remained in profitable operation. Less spectacular operators followed the footsteps of Honest Harry to the redwood country to erect sawmills and drape the eighty-foot seacoast cliffs with spindly loading chutes. William Richardson built a mill at Albion, three or four miles south of Big River, and soon added another at Noyo, seven miles north. The Albion operation did well, but the Noyo mill was frequently raided by local Indians who resented having the trees of their tribal hunting ground pulled down around their heads and their traditional fishing waters cluttered up with lumber schooners.

Silas Coombs, another State of Maine man with an affinity for tall timber, staked out a claim on the Little River and wrote letters home extolling the virtues of his forest paradise. Numerous friends and kinfolk came West to join him and the result was another transplanted New England village, Little River, complete with sawmill, two loading chutes and even a small wharf. Like the Popes and Talbots,

Coombs and his associates preferred to ship their lumber in their own ships and a fleet of thirteen two and three-masted schooners was built at Little River for that purpose.

Before the turn of the century the California coast between San Francisco and Humboldt Bay boasted more than half a hundred redwood lumber "ports," most of them only vague indentations or shallow rivermouth coves on the rocky lee shore. The apron chute and, in later years, the wire cable chute, made ship loading precariously possible at Mendocino, Newport, Gualala, Cleone, Greenwood, Albion, Caspar, Noyo, Hardy Creek and a score of other dog hole ports.

The dawn of a new century brought with it a new concept of logging, based largely on the fact that this is an industry closely tied to the science of transportation. In the pioneer days almost anyone could get an ox-team and an ax and go into the logging business, but as competition and technology increased it required large amounts of capital to build logging railroads, finance steam donkey engines and install modern, mass production mill machinery. It was inevitable that a few big companies should largely supplant the host of small, independent lumbermen who had pioneered the redwood coast.

The Union Lumber Company was one of these, with its headquarters and principal mill established at Fort Bragg in 1885. A railroad was built into the big timber country of the Noyo River watershed, an efficient lumber-loading wharf was constructed and a fleet of steam schooners, the National Steamship Company, was formed to handle passenger and cargo shipments between San Francisco and the company's northern ports.

The earthquake and fire which demolished San Francisco was duplicated on a smaller scale at Fort Bragg, with Union's mill knocked off its foundation and much of the town wrecked, but Captain Hammar of the company's steam schooner *National City* directed the stringing of fire hose to his ship's pumps and saved several of the town's major buildings. A logging locomotive was found wtih steam up and the mill pump was connected to its boiler to spray the fire-threatened plant with water from the log pond.

The Union Lumber Company's founder and president, C. R. Johnson, took the *National City* to San Francisco after the Fort Bragg fire was out and proper instructions had been given for the repair of the mill. While the *National City* was busy hauling refugees and relief supplies on San Francisco Bay, C.R. sized up the lumber needs for the rebuilding of San Francisco, San Jose, Santa Barbara and the other earth-stricken cities. Within three months the big Fort Bragg Mill was at full capacity and the Union steam schooners were heading south with high deckloads and low freeboard. By this time the company controlled the Mendocino Lumber Company, which had been founded by Harry Meiggs, as well as other redwood milling and manufacturing plants in northern California.

ROCKS AND WHITE WATER provided a grim lee for the little *Sequoia* as she hung on her anchors and took on redwood ties via the Cleone wire chute. It will be noted that her boats were prudently lowered to deck level in case the worst happened. Little dog hole droughers like the *Sequoia* carried about two-fifths of their cargo in the holds; three fifths as deckload.

GUALA LANDING dropped redwood lumber to the little two-masted schooner below via high-wire made fast to ship's mast. The carriage-block rolled down from the high landing by gravity, and was pulled back by steam winch.

HIGH AND LIGHT, the steam schooner *Port Orford* was entering Eureka harbor for a redwood lumber cargo when this 1940 photograph was taken. Big for a wooden "single-ender," she was built by Kruse & Banks at North Bend in 1917 as the *H. X. Baxter,* was registered at 1293 gross tons.

WHARF LOADING AT LITTLE RIVER began in 1875, above. Coombs, Stickney & Reeves built a mill there in 1863, loading the small two-masted lumber schooners of that era by chute. When the mill was rebuilt following a major fire in 1874, the small wharf and an additional chute were constructed to speed up loading.

Another of the big companies which was to dominate the milling of California redwood was the Pacific Lumber Company, which traces its beginnings to the little Albion mill of 1869. It began to expand after 1898 when lumberman and ship operator Charles Nelson became president. The third of the redwood "Big Three," the Hammond Lumber Company, took over the Vance Redwood Lumber Company mills and logging railroads in 1890.

Like the mill towns of the Puget Sound country, those of the redwood coast were lively spots, particularly during the traditional loggers' holidays over the Fourth of July and Christmas. Finns predominated among the redwood loggers, while Swedes and Norwegians dominated the Douglas fir forests of Washington and Oregon, but a logger hell-bent for a celebration is much the same the world over.

Most of the early timber companies went all-out to get back as much of the loggers' paychecks as possible as rapidly as possible. They began by cashing the checks at the company store or hotel at a five or ten per cent discount. Since most of the redwood lumber towns were even more isolated than the mill ports of Puget Sound, the boys had little choice but to spend what was left of their six months' wages at company store, hotel and saloon. The only service provided free was the ride back to the woods by logging train when the last dollar had been spent.

At Albion, where the proprietors followed the line of Cyrus Walker and barred saloons from the town, an enterprising businessman bought a lot across the river where he operated a bar of sorts. His bar whiskey was said to be composed of one part the real thing, five parts water and a handful of plug tobacco in the keg to give it flavor and "bite." He is said to have made a fortune and retired to an ornate mansion on Nob Hill.

But, like the mill ports to the north, the Mendocino timber towns began to fade away when the forests were cut back to such distances from the coast that it was no longer profitable to transport logs to the mill and lumber down the coast by schooner. Greenwood, home port of two of the first of the old sailing schooners converted to steam, *Alcatraz* and *Alcazar,* lost its lease on life when the mill shut down in 1929. The 150-foot high loading chute and trestle has fallen into the sea and ships no longer ride at anchor in the doubtful lee of Casket Rock.

The mill at Mendocino City closed down permanently during the depression years. There is no trace left of the mill and loading chutes at Little River or Noyo or Needle Rock.

Redwood lumber is still cut in the sawmills of northern California, but it is shipped by rail or by big trucks along the coastal highway. The steam schooners of the coastwise lumber fleet have vanished from the dog holes of Mendocino as they have from all the other once roaring sawdust cities of the western frontier.

CRUEL ROCKS OF THE MENDOCINO COAST were challenged by the tiny 250-ton *Alcatraz* for thirty years as she shuttled lumber between the dog hole ports of northern California and San Francisco, but the law of averages caught up with her in 1917 when she stranded at Greenwood and was knocked to pieces by the sea.

LAST LUMBER CARGO to leave Grays Harbor under sail went out aboard the bark *Kiaulani* early in World War II. These historic photographs of the big windjammer make sail off the Grays Harbor bar were taken by Bob Cummings of the *Post-Intelligencer*.

Chapter 5

OCEAN AND INTERCOASTAL

SAN FRANCISCO's gold rush boom was, by 1854, degenerating into a bust. Real estate and building activity had reached a feverish peak. Land prices had become ridiculously inflated and credit was strained to the breaking point. The mining industry could no longer sustain the boom economy it had produced. Trouble was in the offing.

Honest Harry Meiggs, ex-alderman and civic benefactor, gave a push to the city's tottering economic structure when he climbed aboard the bark *American* before dawn on October 4, 1854 and sailed on a one-way voyage to Tahiti. He left town owing upwards of a million dollars and the victims of his financial swindles found themselves suddenly staring bankruptcy in the face.

A few months later the first of San Francisco's banks closed its doors and a high official of another, apparently seeing the handwriting on the wall, departed hastily for Australia carrying a satchel which allegedly contained some two million dollars of his bank's assets. The immediate result was a run on the remaining banks. Even Wells Fargo, which was considered immune to the worst financial storms, was forced to lock its doors for a while.

West Notus loading at Tacoma.

Lumber prices, of course, took a header along with everything else. Common lumber, which had sold for $300.00 a thousand in 1850 was down to $24.00 . . . three dollars a thousand less than it cost Pope and Talbot to mill it and ship it down from Puget Sound. The San Francisco market had been able to absorb almost all of the fir and pine lumber exported from the Pacific Northwest, as well as the northern California redwood, so it was essential that lumbermen who wished to survive move fast toward securing new markets.

The first cargo for Australia was shipped from Port Gamble in September of 1854 aboard the Talbot-owned bark *Ella Francis*. Before the end of the year the Puget Sound mills had dispatched cargos of lumber to Hawaii, Sydney, Melbourne, Hong Kong, Tahiti and Valpariso.

Early attempts to sell California redwood on the Australian market met with less success. According to the records of the Mendocino mill, from which the first cargo was shipped, "The trouble with the lumber arose in the first place from the color, for the people there were very conservative; and in the next instance from the fact that all their nails came from England, and were pointed from the head down on all sides. Of course these nails, no matter how they were driven relative to the grain of the wood, acted as a wedge and split the boards, which confirmed the condemnation of this 'blarsted stuff'.

"But as the years went on, and the market was at times depleted of other woods, and lumber of some kind must be had, small lots were disposed of and some of the good qualities of the wood began to be known and appreciated. And still later, when cut nails from the United States came into use, redwood increased in favor, and our original loss opened the door for the larger and more profitable markets now enjoyed by the shippers to that country."

LUMBER PORTS: S. S. *Pacific* topping off deck cargo for Honolulu, Seattle, 1912, above. *Oridono Maru,* lower left, being assisted to berth at Olympia by steam tug *Prospector,* 1927. *Munleon,* McCormick liner, lower right, discharging Columbia River lumber cargo at San Francisco, 1930.

One of the ships launched at East Machias for the Puget Sound—Australian trade was the *Jenny Ford,* which Pope and Talbot advertised as a "clipper three-mast schooner" and carried on their records as a bark. Actually she was neither, being of a new-fangled rig which had not yet been given a name, square-rigged on the foremast, fore-and-aft rigged on main and mizzen.

The *Jenny Ford* was the first barkentine to join the West Coast lumber fleet. Ships of this rig, which combined some of the long-haul qualities of a square-rigger with a schooner's ability to handle with a small crew, became extremely popular in both the coastwise and offshore lumber trade. The last of the breed, the barkentine *Conqueror,* made her last voyage from Olympia and other Puget Sound ports

GREEK FREIGHTER *Ioannis P. Goulandris,* above, loaded full cargo for European delivery at Nettleton mill, Seattle, 1958. *West Notus,* lower left, of McCormick's Pacific Argentine Brazil Line loading lumber for South America at Tacoma, 1940. Steam tug *John Cudahy,* lower right, helps dock offshore lumber carrier at Grays Harbor mill dock, circa 1920.

in 1927 with a cargo of lumber for Durham and Port Elizabeth, South Africa. Although the barkentine rig was a compromise and not designed for maximum speed, the old *Conqueror* averaged better than 230 miles a day for twenty days on her last passage under sail.

The opening of the Panama Canal cut deeply into the fleet of wind ships which had hauled Pacific Coast lumber around the long Cape Horn road to Europe and the East Coasts of the United States and South America. Tramp steamers could carry bigger cargos through the canal more efficiently and infinitely faster than the windjammers. The Big Ditch even made it possible for the little coastal steam schooners to compete to some extent with the deep-water sailing ships. On July 31, 1915 the Grays Harbor marine news carried this item:

"The steam schooner *Willapa* is loading 750,000 feet of spruce lumber at the American mill for Havana, Cuba. This is the first cargo of lumber sent from Grays Harbor to that island. The voyage is expected to take 70 days. The opening of the Panama Canal permits a steamer of the small capacity of the *Willapa* to make the voyage."

The trans-Pacific lumber trade remained the last refuge of sailing ships seeking offshore lumber cargos, but time was running out for them here too. When Japan set about building a merchant marine the era of steam had arrived and the ubiquitous Japanese tramp freighter was soon competing with the elderly sailing ships of western nations for long-haul cargos across the Pacific. The end of World War I placed millions of tons of surplus steel steamships on the market at bargain prices and the last of the big sailing ships headed for the shipbreakers' yards or for lay-up anchorages in harbor backwaters.

LOADING LUMBER on the Luckenbach liner *Harry Luckenbach* at Seattle, 1941.

L
LUCKENBACH

PUGET SOUND LUMBER FOR THE FAR EAST aboard the Liberty-type freighter *Oregon Trader.*

The last voyage made by a lumber-carrying square-rigger from a Pacific Coast port was made in July of 1941 by the old Alaska Packers' bark *Star of Finland,* built at Bath, Maine in 1899. Under her original name of *Kaiulani,* she took the lumber from Grays Harbor around Cape Horn to South America. The shortage of merchant ship tonnage brought on by another world war had brought the old iron bark out of retirement for a last bout with the Cape Horn storms, but her career under canvas was brief. After a single voyage her masts were removed and she became a lumber barge in the Philippine Islands.

The age of sail ended when the *Kaiulani* dropped her tug off the Grays Harbor bar and faded into the sea mist of the North Pacific, the last of all the thousands of her kind that had carried West Coast lumber to the ports of all the world.

Today's lumber cargos are loaded aboard steel steam and motor ships, most of them capable of carrying ten times the 750,000-foot loads which were the average for the wooden steam schooners of fifty years ago.

The bulk of the intercoastal lumber trade is carried on by the steamship fleets of two logging companies, Pope and Talbot and Weyerhaeuser and by States Marine, Luckenbach and Calmar Line freighters.

The *Maru* ships of the Japanese merchant navy, which were almost the only engine-driven competition to the offshore windjammers in the lumber trade a few decades ago, have been joined by the big freighters of a dozen maritime nations at the mill docks of the Pacific Northwest. Their decks piled high in traditional lumber-hauling style, the new ships do the work that was once the refuge of tall windjammers; *Palmyra, Balclutha, Dashing Wave, Forest Pride* and an uncounted host of others. And if the new ships lack something of beauty and romance they have come a long way in providing speed, efficiency and a degree of comfort for their crews that would have amazed—and no doubt delighted—the iron men who sailed the wooden ships of the old-time lumber fleet.

Chapter 6

SHIPS OF STEEL

THE first of the little wooden lumber schooners converted to steam . . . *Newport, Alcazar, Laguna, Alcatraz* and the others . . . were less than two hundred feet long and boasted a gross tonnage of two to three hundred. The engines of those steam schooners of the 1880's were little compound rigs which seldom developed much more than a hundred horsepower, using steam from a single modest Scotch boiler. By festooning the deck with lumber to the level of the wheel house they might be able to haul as much as 300,000 feet of cargo down the coast.

During the forty years that followed there was progress in steam schooner design, but the changes were less revolutionary than might have been expected. The first vessels launched with engines were built with typical sailing schooner hulls and flat sterns, just as the early automobiles came equipped with whip-sockets and other horse and buggy fittings. As builders began to concede that steam, not sail, was the principal source of power, the hull lines of the steam schooners changed accordingly with considerable increase in carrying capacity.

The first steam schooners all had their engines and deckhouses aft . . . "stem-winders" was their unofficial classification. The steering wheel had always been on the stern of the sailing schooners and it was tough enough getting the hard-headed skippers to accept the general idea of steam without further upsetting them by removing them from their traditional place of command. Besides, it was only possible to enter some of the Mendocino dog holes with tiny ships that needed very little water under their bows. And when the clapperman, up on the loading chute, started aiming timber at the plunging deck of a schooner riding the tall Pacific swells far below him, he needed all the uncluttered loading space possible.

Some of the later steam schooners, designed for the longer coastwise run between deep-water Pacific Northwest ports and San Francisco, had engines and deckhouses installed amidships, with runways through the midship house to provide for the stowage of long timbers on deck. Like the stem-winders, the double-enders were expected to carry at least half their load as deck cargo.

McCormick liner *Wallingford* at San Francisco.

The last wooden steam schooner ever built was the *Esther Johnson,* launched at the Matthews yard in Portland in 1923 for A. B. Johnson. She was a double-ender of 1104 gross tons, 208 feet long and with a carrying capacity of 1,250,000 board feet of lumber. Her triple expansion engine and two water-tube boilers provided her with 825 working horsepower.

There had been a few larger wooden lumber carriers launched. The Hart-Wood Lumber Company's *San Diego,* built by Mathews at Hoquiam in 1918, was registered at 1487 gross tons and was an amazing 240 feet in length. And there was McCormick's *Everett,* 237 feet long and 1751 gross tons, built at the McCormick yard in St. Helens in 1920. These giants of the steam schooner fleet had explored the outer reaches of size and carrying capacity, for there are definite limits beyond which practical wooden

ship design cannot go. A wooden hull is not a rigid fabric but a joining-together of thousands of component parts into a resilient whole. This resiliency of a wooden ship becomes audible when the going is heavy in the sound of timbers, hull planks and decking all working against the wood and metal fastenings which keep them in place.

If such a hull is much over two hundred feet in length the leverage of its own size and weight becomes so great that it tends to "hog" as the ends sag and the midships section takes on a humpbacked look. Big inland steamers combated this problem with a network of "hog-chains" above decks which acted like the girders of a bridge to support bow and stern, but such contraptions were impractical for a cargo-carrying ocean ship. The only alternative was an inner network of bracing timbers which would leave little space in the hold for cargo.

On August 16, 1908, the last of a trio of new steam schooners was completed at the Seattle yard of Robert Moran. The *Riverside,* a stemwinder with two masts forward swinging the 70-foot-long cargo booms which were a steam schooner trade mark, steamed sweetly across Elliott Bay and then picked up speed to take the three-mile trial course off Vashon Island at an easy twelve knots. This was two knots above her contract speed, so shipyard manager J. V. Paterson was in a pleasant mood when he joined the "score of guests who partook of a collation served at noon." The *Riverside* had passed her tests with flying colors, as had her sister ships *Falcon,* also built for the Charles Nelson Company and the *Stanley Dollar,* for Robert Dollar. The three Moran-built ships of 1908 were built for the coastwise lumber trade and they were classed as steam schooners, but from keel to pilot house they were built of steel. The days of the wooden steam schooners were numbered.

The new ships of steel were 240 feet long, of 1800 gross tons and could carry better than a million and a half feet of lumber. They could carry other cargos too. The best of the wooden schooners had a tendency to work their seams loose and leak a bit, but the steel ones could, and frequently did, haul grain and other commodities that required dry storage.

Left, top to bottom: Steel steam schooners *Melville Dollar, El Cedro, Brookings* and *Griffdu.*

Right, top to bottom: Steel steam schooners *Paraiso, Alvarado, W. R. Chamberlain, Jr.* and *H. W. Baxter.*

During the next five years the change from wood to steel was rapid. The *Aroline,* built at San Francisco in 1913 for the Independent Steamship Company, was one of the first ships to pass through the Panama Canal. She was chartered in January, 1914 to carry a cargo of creosoted piles from Seattle for the construction of a breakwater at Colon. The little *Aroline,* later Pacific Steamship Company's *Admiral Goodrich* and the National Steamship Company's second *Noyo,* was able to slip through the still incompleted canal with her load of building material before the waterway was officially opened.

Like some of the other early steel lumber carriers, the *Aroline* was built along conventional steam schooner lines and unless you looked closely it was difficult to tell that she was different from her wooden sisters. As the new type evolved further, however, the similarity became more and more remote, until the term steam schooner came to apply to the work in which a ship engaged . . . the coastwise lumber trade . . . rather than to any family resemblance the vessel might have to the old-time sailing droughers.

The *Riverside* made her maiden voyage from Puget Sound to San Francisco, carrying 1,750,000 feet of lumber from Tacoma and Everett. She performed well and made her owners extra profits by performing impromptu salvage operations during the course of later voyages. In October, 1912 the Pacific Coast was beset by a series of violent storms which wrought havoc among the lumber fleet. The steam schooner *Yosemite* had her rudder swept away by a huge sea off the Grays Harbor bar and the *Rochelle,* a former Great Lakes Craft converted to steam schooner rig, took a horrible mauling on the Columbia River bar and staggered back to Astoria with most of her deck cargo gone and the chief engineer standing in water up to his waist to tend the throttle. A few days later the *Daisy Freeman* poked her nose out past the Columbia jetty loaded with 750,000 feet of lumber loaded at Portland for San Francisco. A few hours later the bar tug *Goliath* brought her back inside, her rudder and deck load missing and so badly waterlogged that, except for masts and funnel, she was almost invisible.

During the course of the October storms the *Riverside* came upon the remains of the 400-ton wooden steam schooner *J. J. Loggie* off the coast of northern California. The *Loggie* was so far gone that her crew had already deserted her, but the stout steel *Riverside* rescued the crew, if not the ship.

The following month brought little improvement in the weather. On November 1 the gasoline schooner *Osprey* piled up on the jetty outside Marshfield, Oregon. This was a historic occasion, for it was re-

THE STEAM SCHOONERS GO TO WAR. Wearing battle gray and with deck guns topping off their lumber cargos, many of the coastwise fleet served the nation in World War 2, as they had in 1917 and 1918. The *A. M. Baxter,* above, a 253-foot, 2400-ton single-ender of 1919 vintage, was operated by the Horace X. Baxter Steamship Company of San Francisco.

ported that "a feature of this disaster was the attempt of Silas G. Christofferson, an aviator, to perform rescue work from the air. Accompanied by a newspaper reporter, the aviator made two trips out to the wreck but was unable to render assistance, the vessel having disappeared with all on board. The aviator afterward expressed the opinion that a properly equipped aeroplane might someday do effective work in such cases." The power barkentine *Archer* was dismasted off the Oregon coast shortly thereafter and even the big German bark *R. C. Rickmers* lost most of her sails and a number of deck fittings while trying to make the Columbia to load a two and a half million foot cargo of Oregon lumber for Europe.

The *Riverside,* making her return voyage up the coast, was again in the center of activity. A hundred miles off the Washington coast the *Riverside* sighted the sad remains of the schooner *Oceania Vance*. The *Vance* had been en route from the Columbia River to San Diego when the storm caught up with her. When the *Riverside* came along the little wooden schooner had only her foremast standing, her rigging in a hopeless tangle, her seams open, her hull strained and her deck load cluttering up the sealanes from Cape Flattery to Cape Blanco. Her cook was nonchalantly cooking dinner over a bonfire on the poop, however, and her skipper was scornful of the *Riverside's* proffered tow. The eight men of the crew rebelled at this, feeling that it was carrying the traditional "firmness" of a Scandinavian Navy skipper to the point of downright stubbornness. They forced the captain to take a line from the *Riverside* and the battered *Oceania Vance* was towed safely to Port Townsend.

The fine performance of the *Riverside* and her sister ships prompted even the more conservative steam schooner operators to add new steel ships to their fleets, although the *Riverside* proved she was not entirely immune to the fate of her wooden sisters by striking Blunt's Reef on a clear June night in 1913 and sinking with great rapidity.

By that time it was obvious that the steel steam schooner far exceeded its wooden prototype in efficiency and the marine pages of West Coast newspapers were full of accounts of new ones entering the trade. The *William Chatham,* built by Union Iron Works at San Francisco in 1912 was hauling big

LUMBER LADY, above, of a World War 1 type similar to the *Baxter,* was built at Ecorse, Michigan in 1918 as the *Cottonplant.* After World War 2 service she went back to hauling lumber between Rainier, Oregon and San Pedro for the Van Fleet Lumber Company until the big Rainier mill burned down in 1955. *Lumber Lady* was the last steam schooner to be privately operated by a West Coast lumber company.

The old Umpqua bar tug *Gleaner* brought hundreds of lumber schooners safe to port in times of peace. (See page 25.) During the last war she worked out of the Seattle Port of Embarkation, helped send them off on hazardous wartime voyages, lower right.

cargos between Grays Harbor, Willapa Harbor, Puget Sound and San Francisco for the Loop Lumber Company of Aberdeen. In May of 1913 the *Oliver J. Olson* made her first voyage from San Francisco to Tacoma. A few months later the steel *Melville Dollar,* following the traditional steam schooner custom of making a bit of extra money by acting as a towboat, was reported bringing the Yukon River stern-wheeler *La Velle Young* down to Seattle to be dismantled. Even Fred Linderman, who had declined to join Dollar and Nelson in their 1908 steel ship construction project, had added the steel *Cricket* to his "Insect Line" by 1913.

Linderman congratulated himself that, if nothing else, he wouldn't have to worry about the *Cricket* catching on fire, a constant hazard to wooden ships like his *Bee, Wasp* and *Hornet.* Interestingly enough, the fire-resistant *Cricket,* substituting an asphalt cargo for her usual load of lumber, caught fire at a Portland dock in 1914 and burned to the waterline. She was rebuilt, however, and was seen on Puget Sound as late as 1954, loading lumber for South America under Peruvian ownership.

As early as 1912 West Coast maritime journals were documenting the revolutionary changes in the steam schooner fleet. The following account, date-

STEEL STEAM SCHOONER *St. Helens,* above, was diverted from Puget Sound—California lumber trade in 1911 to haul general cargo to Nome and other far northern ports, operated by E. J. Dodge Company of San Francisco. She's pictured above headed for Nome, her deck loaded with six scows, three launches, four horseboats and 300,000 feet of lumber.

Below, steel coasters *Eldorado* and *Nann Smith.*

Opposite page, top to bottom: *Mt. Baker, Eureka* and *Tallac.*

lined San Francisco, September 30, 1912, is typical:

"With the addition of the latest steam schooners, a number of them of steel construction, to the big fleet operating between San Francisco, Seattle and other Pacific Coast ports a complete revolution has been brought about. Where formerly the size of these steam schooners seldom exceeded 200 net tons, the new additions are nearly as big as the regular liners.

"The small craft of the past were provided with unsatisfactory passenger accommodation, which failed to attract patronage except from persons compelled to patronize the only vessels sailing to some of the lesser ports. This condition is now gradually undergoing a change, and it is now possible to sail to most of the smaller ports on vessels which, though listed as steam schooners, possess features such as previously were only found on the big steamships. Smok-

ing and lounging rooms as well as good sized promenade decks are among the luxuries provided.

"Wilson Brothers announced yesterday that the steam schooner *Columbia,* recently completed on the Atlantic and now steaming toward San Francisco, is passing through Magellan and is expected to arrive here in thirty days. The *Columbia,* a steel craft of 1,188 tons set, has first-class accommodations for 65 passengers and the steerage will accommodate fifteen additional. She will be operated between San Francisco and Grays Harbor or Seattle and is expected to prove a welcome addition to the vessels now operating.

"Olson & Mahoney are having the new steamship *Californian* constructed which will be placed on the San Francisco-Portland run. The new vessel, which will be completed and ready for operation the first of the year, is 250 feet in length, 21 feet beam and will carry about 2,500 tons of freight, or about 2,000,000 feet of lumber. The passenger accommodations, which will number about sixty for the first class, are to be placed amidships and will in many respects rival those of the regular passenger liners, and the promenade deck will be considerably larger.

"Charles R. McCormick & Co. are having two new steamships constructed at St. Helens and W. S. Scammell & Co. are preparing to place other new

Henry T. Scott.

Admiral Goodrich.

George Olson.

Cricket.

TALL DECKLOADS AND LONG CARGO BOOMS were in the steam schooner tradition as the *Hamlin F. McCormick* topped off her load of fir logs at Seattle about 1938. This was one of the McCormick Steamship Company's first World War 1-built steel intercoastal carriers, purchased in 1923.

vessels on different runs along the coast. Practically every concern operating out of San Francisco is preparing to care for the big increase in business in the freight and passenger line.

"Although the combined passenger traffic of the steam schooner concerns along the coast is only about three percent of the total volume of business, this amounts to a pretty figure at the end of each year. Up to about eighteen months ago there was keen competition and the city was overrun with petty agents who sought to obtain trade for the vessels they represented without any particular regard to making true statements.

"This proved so unsatisfactory that the steam schooner owners got together and established an agency which now handles the sale of transportation on these small vessels exclusively. This not only saves the owners a lot of good cash, but has also resulted in removing the stigma of fraud, which was sometimes charged against the former agents.

"Thousands of persons who are not pressed for time prefer to travel on the smaller vessels, which gives them an opportunity to spend more time at sea and, incidentally, saves a bit of money, for the fare charged on the steam schooners is considerably less than charged by the big liners".

While the passenger-carrying sideline was promoted by most owners, (Fred Linderman said they were more trouble than they were worth and refused to carry them on his "Insect Line"), their principal purpose was still the hauling of lumber. Here, too, the new steel ships proved their capabilities. On April 25, 1914, the Grays Harbor marine news included this item:

"All local and probably all coast records for speed in loading lumber carriers were broken in the completion of the steel steam schooner *Francis H. Leggett,* after 20 hours of work. The *Leggett* carried

LURLINE BURNS operated in Puget Sound–California lumber trade under the houseflag of the Burns Steamship Company of San Francisco. A 290-footer of 2800 gross tons, she was built at Portland in 1918 as the *Caddopeak.*

1,470,000 feet of lumber from Hoquiam to San Pedro. The steamer was in the harbor but 25 hours. Thirty men were used in loading railroad ties."

On July 18 came word of another fast loading operation by a big steel steam schooner at Grays Harbor:

"After a trifle over 27 hours loading, the steamer *John A. Hooper* with 2,350,000 feet of railroad ties, cleared this afternoon, breaking in one trip three records for fast loading for a single shipment of ties, and the largest domestic shipment ever to leave the harbor. The *Hooper* will cross the bar drawing 20 feet. She arrived Thursday morning at 11 o'clock and on departing had been in the harbor 53 hours. She did not load overtime and during the course of loading moved from the Grays Harbor Lumber Co. mill in Hoquiam to the Aberdeen Lumber & Shingle Company, Aberdeen. The best known loading record ever made by a steam vessel was that of the *Francis H. Leggett,* which took on approximately a million and a half feet of lumber and cleared in 25 hours. This is believed to be a world's record. The *Leggett* worked overtime and her record cannot be compared to that of the *Hooper* in time of actual loading. The largest previous cargo of railroad ties to leave this port has not exceeded a million feet. Locally the cargo of the *Hooper* has been exceeded only by foreign tramp vessels going to foreign ports. Her destination is San Pedro."

Steel was definitely on the way up, although in that year of 1914 the coastwise steam schooner fleet still consisted of 160 wooden ships and only 28 steel-hulled ones. Until the beginning of the great depression in 1929 there were still almost a hundred of the little wooden schooners working the West Coast lumber ports, but by then they were fighting a truly losing battle. Other economic facts of life than bank failures and a depressed lumber market were driv-

LAKER OUT OF TACOMA. *Lake Frances* was one of the World War 1 freighters of which many were adapted to the lumber schooner trade. Formerly operated by the Ford Motor Company's short-lived steamship line, she's pictured here leaving Tacoma harbor in the service of the Coastal Steamship Company of Tacoma, 1940.

ing them to lay-up moorages in droves.

The end of the first world war brought with it a tremendous surplus of almost new steel ships constructed during the wartime crash program of the War Shipping Administration. The government made many of these vessels available to American Flag operators at prices as low as one twentieth of actual construction costs. Coastwise ship owners found that one type of war-built ship, the so-called "Lakers", were almost ideal for the lumber trade. These small freighters, all named after American lakes, were approximately 250 feet long and of slightly over 2000 gross tonnage. Their reciprocating steam engines, which developed from 1200 to 1400 horsepower, were economical to operate and their maximum loaded depth of about twenty feet made it possible for them to negotiate the major West Coast lumber-shipping ports without difficulty.

Only moderate changes in design were required to convert them to highly efficient "steam schooners", although that terminology had now lost much of its original meaning. The two conventional freighter masts were replaced by four, one each at the break of forecastle and poop; the other two amidships at either end of the deckhouse. Like the pre-war steam schooners, these masts were equipped with oversize cargo booms much longer than those of a conventional freighter. These 70 to 75 foot booms speeded loading and discharging, for they could lift loads of five tons and provided maximum handling range for the stevedores who operated them. A steam schooner could tie up at a mill dock and, with her long-armed reach, pick up cargo over a wide area without repeated shifting of position.

The "Lakers" soon dominated the coastwise lumber trade. The last of the McCormick wooden steam schooners, *Wapama* and *Celilo* were sold as the wartime freighters took over the company's coastal routes. Larger "West"-class ships formed the backbone of McCormick's Pacific Argentine Brazil Line on the South American run. The Pacific Lumber Company found that the *Lake Galewood* could handle the Humboldt Bay, San Francisco, San Diego lumber business and she went to work renamed *Scotia,* after the 181-ton wooden schooner of 1888 vintage. Schafer Brothers Logging Company of Grays Harbor put three of the wartime-built ships in service as the *Anna, Hubert* and *Margaret Schafer.*

SUNSET ON PUGET SOUND and the Oliver J. Olson Company's *George Olson* is leaving the Port of Seattle for another coastwise voyage to California.

S.S. *Peter Helms,* right, was photographed while preparing to discharge at the Port of Stockton in 1933. Built at Mobile in 1920 as the *Hutchinson* operated in McCormick Steamship Company and Pope & Talbot service from 1929 until 1948.

ON THE BEACH, the McCormick Steamship Company's South American lumber carrier *West Mahwah* became a total loss as a result of this 1937 stranding. An 8500-ton "three-islander" of World War I vintage, the *West Mahwah* was typical of the steel Shipping Board freighters diverted to the lumber trade in the 1920's.

AT DOCK IN SAN FRANCISCO, the McCormick steamer *Munleon* was photographed in 1930 following a coastwise voyage from Portland and Longview. She was lost at sea late the following year.

LOADING FROM DOCK AND SCOWS, two big intercoastal freighters gobble up multi-million foot lumber loads at Olympia. Olympic Steamship Company's *Olympic Pioneer* is in the foreground, with the Weyerhaeuser Steamship Company's *F. S. Bell in* the background.

Most of the steel steam schooners and a few of the old wooden ones went to war again after December 7, 1941. Many of them did not return and those that did found slim pickings in the lumber business. Mills, once all located close to tidewater, had followed the receding timber inland. Rail and highway transportation had taken over the lion's share of lumber shipments. The era of the coastwise lumber schooner was all but ended.

The wooden steam schooners *Svea, Idaho* and *Oregon* had dozed away the war years on rotten row, the mudflats of Oakland Creek. The old *Wapama,* renamed *Tongass,* had served until 1947 on the Alaska freight and passenger routes, but then she was tied up in Lake Union to await junking. The *Svea, Idaho* and *Oregon,* after waiting twenty years for sailing orders that never came, were broken up for scrap in the fall of 1950. McCormick's old *Wapama,* slowly rotted at her Seattle mooring until, in 1958, the California Division of Beaches and Parks purchased her to be added to the maritime museum fleet on the San Francisco waterfront. The last of her colorful clan, the *Wapama* will survive as a memorial to the brave little ships of the "Scandinavian Navy". With her is the three-masted wooden schooner *C. A. Thayer* and the iron-hulled square-rigger *Balclutha,* which once sailed the Pacific with cargos of Pope and Talbot lumber.

The few remaining coastwise lumber carriers . . . the Oliver J. Olson Company, formerly Olson & Mahoney, is the largest operator remaining . . . have lost the last of their family resemblance to the old-time steam schooners. The tall masts and long booms that were once considered the last word in efficiency have given way to far less salty, but still more efficient loading gear.

In 1952 the *Mary Olson* was the last of the Olson coastwise lumber fleet to be converted to a packaged lumber carrier. Her tall masts and booms were replaced by two motor-cranes perched amidships at bridge level. The cab-enclosed cranes are similar to the kind seen on shoreside construction jobs and look more out of place at sea than did the stove-pipe funnels of the old converted sailing schooners.

But their use permits the loading of full carrier-loads of lumber, thus eliminating the old fashioned method of stowing cargo piece by piece. The steam schooners had always been willing to compromise a bit when their survival was at stake, and through that willingness to change with the times a few descendants of the "Scandinavian Navy" still ply their trade along the West Coast of the United States.

BRIDGE-FULL AND BACKING OUT, the *Dorothy Wintermote,* ex-*Lake Cayuga* of World War 1 vintage, leaves her Seattle pier en-route to San Francisco, 1937.

OLD-TIME STEAM SCHOONER CARGO BOOMS, like those formerly used on the *Barbara Olson*, above, have given way to self-powered motor cranes like those pictured on the opposite page.

DONKEYMAN ALLEGES BRUTAL TREATMENT

FILES CHARGE AGAINST SCHOONER'S CREW.

Sailor Says He Was Driven Ashore From Lottie Bennett at Valparaiso, Chile.

1914

Victim of a system of hazing which he says is practiced aboard the vessel at sea, beaten and tortured by officers and members of the crew, and finally driven ashore at Valparaiso under threat of death, was the experience of James Oliver, donkey engineer of the American schooner Lottie Bennett, according to a complaint made by Oliver to the United States commissioner of navigation, Washington, D. C., and forwarded to United States Shipping Commissioner William Welsh of Tacoma for investigation.

A reign of terror prevailed during the entire voyage with the mate acting the stellar role, according to Oliver in his charges filed against the officers of the schooner.

International Fray.

That the troubles some times aboard the Lottie Bennett were in the nature of an international fray is shown in the roster of the vessel, as given by Oliver. He explained that the captain was a Swede, the mate a Russian Finn and the crew consisted of two Germans, a Norwegian, an Englishman and himself.

"I was the only American aboard and they all took turns to abuse me," said Oliver. "When I was not the butt of their jokes and the victim of their hazing practices, the Englishman was at their mercy.

"They made the ship a perfect hell day and night. The mate, with a revolver in each hand, kept strutting about the deck and at all times wore brass knuckles ready to knock down any member of the crew who was in his way."

Another Badly Beaten.

Oliver states that on April 6 the Englishman, while at the wheel, was knocked down, both eyes blackened and his nose broken by the mate, who attacked him without the least provocation. He says that he and the Englishman were told they would be driven ashore at Valparaiso and threatened with death if they remained aboard after the Lottie Bennett reached port on the Chilean coast.

The Lottie Bennett has loaded here on many occasions. She is now en route from Valparaiso to the Columbia river.

Left, top to bottom: *North Pacific,* Northland Transportation Company, *Cascade,* E. K. Wood Lumber Company and *Anna Schafer,* Schafer Bros. Logging Company of Aberdeen.

Right, top to bottom: *Nabesna,* Portland Steamship Company was wartime *Lake Filbert. Margaret Schafer,* formerly the *Corsicana* and *Timberman,* Schafer Bros., *Karen Olson,* Oliver J. Olson Company. *Montanan,* Hawaiian-American Line.

GREAT SHOWING BY PUGET SOUND

It Stands Next to New York in Tonnage Cleared and Entered at Customs Houses in Fiscal Year of 1913.

5,945,826 TONS OF SHIPPING REPORTED

PORT TOWNSEND, Saturday, July 25.—According to the Statistical Abstract of the United States, prepared by the department of foreign and domestic commerce for the fiscal year ending June 30, 1913, the port of Puget Sound comes next to the port of New York in the entire United States in tonnage cleared and entered at the customs houses. For the year cited, entrance tonnage of Puget Sound amounted to 2,887,322 tons, with clearances of 3,058,504 tons, a total shipping business of 5,945,826 tons passing through the customs department of Puget Sound. New York continues in the lead of all world's ports and makes the tremendous showing of 28,834,780 tons, of which clearances amounted to 14,370,619 tons and entrances to 14,464,161 tons.

Next to tonnage volume of Puget Sound is the port of New Orleans, with entrances of 2,545,241 tons and clearances of 2,766,775 tons, a total tonnage business of 5,312,016 tons. Philadelphia takes fourth place, with a total tonnage of 5,108,600 tons, entrances being 2,069,111 and clearances of 2,274,625 tons. For the same year the report shows a total tonnage business for San Francisco of 2,278,532 tons, entrances being 1,007,796 tons and clearances of 1,270,736 tons, a tonnage business for 1913 less by 3,667,294 tons than that of the port of Puget Sound.

Figures for the calendar year of 1912 are used in the Statistical Abstract for showing the tonnage business of ports of Europe and Asia, and while they do not cover the same twelve months of the business of American ports, they include half of the same year and half of the preceding year. An examination of these figures shows that for the calendar year of 1912 the port of Hamburg came second to the port of New York, with a total tonnage volume of 27,404,989 tons. Rotterdam followed among the ports of Europe, with a total tonnage of 23,084,277, and next in line was Antwerp, with a total tonnage of 22,937,073 tons. London is represented with a tonnage of 19,548,724 and Liverpool follows with a total tonnage trade of 14,699,889.

For the year 1912 the prominent ports of Asia recorded a heavy tonnage traffic and among these the British port of Hongkong leads with a total tonnage of 21,614,995. These figures are exclusive of Chinese junks, which represented quite an impressive tonnage capacity. Shanghai, handling the traffic of the Yangtsze Valley, shows a total tonnage of 18,642,803. Singapore recorded 16,444,246 tons; Kobe, Japan, 12,134,312 tons and Yokohama, Janan, 7,591,439 tons.

SUNSET SAILING of latter day Olson "steam schooner" above, symbolizes the last days of the coastwise lumber steamers. The Oliver J. Olson Company, last survivor of the old wooden lumber schooner operators, now concentrates on barge operations, below, has only two self-propelled lumber carriers in service.

CLATTER OF STEAM WINCHES is no longer a mark of lumber loading operations. Long cargo booms and winches powered by steam from ship's boilers have given way to individually powered motor cranes, like those of the *C-Trader,* aboard remaining lumber-carrying steamers and barges of the coastwise fleet.

DOWN TO THE SEA BY BARGE. Many timber shipments are now moved by towed barges, some of them highly specialized. Island Tug & Barge Company's self-unloading log barge *Island Fir* is shown in action on the opposite page. Crown-Zellerbach's *Crown #1*, above, can handle as much lumber as could a fleet of the little wooden steam schooners of fifty years ago. Covered barges like those at the right haul paper pulp for Powell River Ltd. Other Island Tug self-unloading timber barges are pictured below, *Island Maple,* left, *Island Logger,* right.

Chapter 7

THE SEA IS CRUEL

Wreck of the *Kvichak*.

IN the late fall of 1899 the three-masted schooner *American Girl* slipped out of the Golden Gate and headed north off the lightship, toward Port Hadlock, Washington for a cargo of lumber. Off the Oregon coast she fell in with a November storm of near-hurricane force. Off the grim headland of Cape Flattery the bark *Highland Light* sighted the *American Girl* briefly, driving toward the northwest with a single foresail set. The *Highland Light* reached the shelter of Juan de Fuca Strait with sails blown to shreds and bulkheads stove in, but the *American Girl* and her eight-man crew had vanished completely.

In April, 1906, the halibut steamer *New England* was headed toward Vancouver from the fishing banks when her lookout sighted the bleached bones of a wrecked ship piled up in a remote bay on the east shore of one of the Queen Charlotte Islands. The wreckage was identified as that of the *American Girl,* but no trace of her crew was ever found.

Such mysterious tragedies were frequent—almost commonplace—in the early days of the coastwise and offshore lumber ships. Such electronic aids as radar, gyro-compass, direction finder and radio were, of course, undreamed of by the hard-bitten sailors of that age. When a ship lost sight of land it lost all communication with the rest of the world, dependent solely on its own strength and the skill of its crew for survival.

Even the steam schooners which followed the "inside track" on their coastwise runs, five miles off the beach, were all alone if they got into trouble when fog or heavy rain cut visibility and their feeble distress flares couldn't be sighted from shore. Sometimes a disabled ship would drift helplessly for days, just out of the shipping lanes but within a few miles of a major West Coast port. Not infrequently a long-voyage bark or a square-rigger would be sighted drifting helplessly within sight of land, her crew dead or dying of scurvy and with no means of summoning help.

In 1901 the list of West Coast lumber ships, ocean and coastwise, which met disaster read like this:

January 3, Schooner *J. Eppinger* lost on rocks at Fort Ross
January 8, Schooner *Joseph and Henry* stranded Alsea Bay
January 10, Schooner *Fawn* stranded at Grays Harbor
January 31, Schooner *Surprise* lost at sea
February 22, Schooner *Fred Gower* lost at sea
February 20, British ship *Yarora* posted missing at sea
March 3, Schooner *Anna* lost at sea
March 18, Ship *Rathdown* posted missing
March 23, Barkentine *Monitor* foundered off Grays Harbor
March 30, British ship *Cape Wrath* posted missing
June 20, Ship *John McDonald* burned at sea
July 24, Bark *Empire* burned at sea
August 29, British bark *Baroda* stranded off Coquille Harbor
September, British ship *Glenbreck* lost at sea
British ship *Manchester* lost at sea

It will be noted that of all the victims that year were sailing vessels, but by 1913 the list had grown to include a number of steamers, including one of the new steel-hulled steam schooners. There was one notable difference, however. Radio had become standard equipment on many ships . . . the *Yosemite,*

Shoshone, Cascade and *Yellowstone* started the trend among the wooden schooners in 1910 . . . and as a result fewer ships were "posted missing". Even with this miraculous device for summoning help at sea, however, the shipwreck toll of 1913 was a heavy one. The schooner *Americana,* headed for Australia with lumber from the Columbia River, went missing with all hands. She had no power other than the wind and, of course, no radio. The schooner *Aloha* was abandoned off Destruction Island and piled up on the Vancouver Island coast. The schooner *Borealis,* with lumber from Mukilteo for Samoa, was wrecked and abandoned on Tonga Island. The steam schooner *Charles Nelson,* laden with 750,000 feet of lumber, burned to the waterline at the northern California redwood port of Fields Landing and the steam schooner *Fulton* was stranded on the British Columbia coast. The steel steam schooner *Francis H. Leggett* rammed and sank the wooden schooner *J. H. Lunsmann* in San Francisco harbor; the schooner *Lyman D. Foster,* bound from Bellingham to Levuka with 900,000 feet of lumber, was abandoned off Suva, and the wooden steam schooner *Merced* was stranded at Punta Gorda and became a total loss.

The little steam schooner *Thomas L. Wand* was badly damaged in collision with the freighter *Pleiades;* the *Point Arena* hit the beach at Pigeon Point and was smashed to pieces, and the steel steam schooner *Riverside* sank after crashing into Blunt's Reef.

The schooner *Robert Searles,* out of Astoria with a full cargo of lumber, put in at Kahului totally disabled and with most of her deckload swept away. The underwriters declared her a total loss. The big freighter *Robert Dollar,* heavily laden with Oregon lumber for Shanghai, struck the Columbia bar and was seriously damaged; the steam schooner *Samoa* hit the beach at Point Reyes; the bark *S. C. Allen,* with lumber from Port Ludlow for Honolulu, was wrecked at Diamond Head. The *Stanley Dollar,* steel steam schooner, wandered ashore on Puget Sound, and the two little wooden steam schooners *Temple E. Dorr* and *Yellowstone* rammed each other off Point Arena.

This maritime mayhem took place in a single year and only the misfortunes of those vessels which happened to be carrying Pacific Coast lumber are listed. And a shipwreck, even one involving an humble carrier of railroad ties, shingles or grape stakes, is usually more serious than the bare statistics indicate. Especially if you happen to be involved in it.

In the good old days, when government was reluctant to interfere with the inalienable right of the American business man to make the largest possible profit on the smallest possible investment, a seaman signing on a lumber ship was likely to run afoul of an interesting theory held by many of those who owned the ships. The theory held, first, that since lumber is buoyant it was reasonable to heap as much of it as possible on a ship, both below and above decks. Even if the hull ended up a foot or two under water the cargo would keep it afloat. The second point followed logically: since cargos of lumber could keep a ship afloat, almost any superannuated old hulk could be employed in that trade, no matter how far gone in dry-rot and iron sickness.

Like most theories, this one had flaws, as many a deluded sailor discovered to his cost. In the first place, a ship loaded down to the gunwales with cargo until it resembled a sea-going woodpile might not sink, but it was likely to wallow about, refuse to answer its helm properly and end up draped across a jetty or offshore reef. And in the second place, some of the ancient craft placed in the lumber trade were so decrepit that a cargo of pingpong balls couldn't have kept them afloat in any kind of a blow.

The case of the bark *Southern Chief* was a classic example. She was a real old-timer, having put in at Port Townsend for the first time in the early 1850's. She was by no means a new craft then, nor a happy one for the crew. She arrived short-handed on that pioneer voyage, three men having been buried at sea . . . murdered by the captain and mates, according to the remaining foremast hands, four of whom were subsequently shot and clubbed to death in an altercation on the Port Townsend waterfront.

The crews of the *Southern Chief* may not have enjoyed long lives, but the ship did. She made her last voyage from Puget Sound in December, 1894, being then just a few months under fifty years old. Her musty holds and rotten decks were crammed with nearly a million feet of lumber, loaded at Tacoma for Adelaide. Soon after the tug dropped her off Cape Flattery a brisk southeast wind set in to put whitecaps on the long Pacific rollers.

The *Southern Chief* had withstood the pounding of a lot of waves in the course of half a century and now she had reached the end of her endurance. Like the wonderful one-horse shay, she just wore out all at once and, as wind and sea kicked up briskly, she proceeded to fall apart in a truly spectacular manner. Her seams opened wide to welcome aboard the whole Pacific Ocean, her poopdeck came loose and fell overboard and her ancient decks began to undulate, upsetting the donkey engine and boiler which rolled about smashing holes in the bulwarks. The masts fell down and the deckload lashings broke, spilling timbers overboard, some of which knocked her rudder off.

Schooner Cheats Davy Jones Again

Six times the steam schooner Bandon (center) has been wrecked, but each time has been saved from going to the bottom of the sea.

ON THE BEACH. The steam schooner *Caoba,* ex-*Coaster,* was abandoned off the mouth of the Columbia during a 1924 storm. The hulk hit the Long Beach peninsula, where it remained a landmark for many years.

Steam schooner *Bandon* was wrecked seven times in the course of an adventurous career dating from 1905. Newspaper accounts like the one at the left told of her apparently charmed life. Her last brush with disaster was a stranding at Trinidad Head, California in 1941. Shortly thereafter her luck ran out and she was intentionally grounded at her namesake port of Bandon, Oregon and burned for salvage.

It was fortunate for her crew that the *Southern Chief* had chosen to disintegrate within fifty miles of Cape Flattery and well within the shipping lanes. The barkentine *Skagit* came along in time to remove all hands safely and after a while the tugs *Richard Holyoke* and *Sea Lion* towed the wreckage back into Port Townsend Bay. The *Southern Chief* had certainly proven that a lumber cargo would float, for what the tugs brought in was mostly the cargo, with bits of the old bark clinging to it here and there.

A Seattle newspaper sent a reporter to survey the wreckage, publishing this report of his findings:

"The wreck of the *Southern Chief* was today towed into port by the tugs *Richard Holyoke* and *Sea Lion.* The vessel is the most perfect specimen of decayed marine architecture that ever reached Puget Sound. The seas ripped dozens of planks from the

WRECKED ON COOS BAY BAR on June 23, 1944, the *George L. Olson* became a total loss, above. A 223-footer built at Oakland in 1917, she was formerly the *Ryder Hanify*.

GIRLIE MAHONEY, formerly the *James S. Higgins,* built by John Lindstrom at Aberdeen in 1904, ended her career in December, 1919 when an inshore storm battered her against the cliffs in the "harbor" at Albion on the California Redwood Coast, lower right.

ANOTHER VICTIM OF THE COOS BAY BAR was the little wooden steam schooner *Claremont,* first of two coastal lumber carriers to bear that name. Built by Lindstrom at Aberdeen in 1907, the 747-ton *Claremont* missed the channel while inbound in May 22, 1915. In spite of assistance from the S.S. *Breakwater,* at the left in the picture above, the pounding seas soon demolished the *Claremont.*

side of the bark, exposing timbers so rotten that they could be picked to pieces with a jack-knife. Rust and innumerable bolt holes had perforated the ribs of the bark until they resembled teredo-eaten piles. Shipping men and veteran sailors who have braved the storms of many seas in vessels considered unsafe were astonished at the complete rottenness of the *Southern Chief.* Before she sailed from Tacoma the starboard anchor and 40 fathoms of chain were lost overboard. Then the bark went to sea with only one kedge anchor of 2500 pounds, which would not have held a vessel of her size in a heavy wind or sea. Below the deck, hidden by nicely painted boards, there was not a sound timber or rib in the hull.

"That was the condition of the bark when the owners permitted 15 persons to hazard their lives and incidentally risk loss of a cargo worth $10,000 by going on a deepwater voyage to a foreign port 4000 miles distant. It must also be remembered that it was only a year or two ago the vessel was engaged in the San Francisco-Puget Sound coal trade, making voyages that increased the danger tenfold."

The journalistic indignation aroused by the collapse of the *Southern Chief* had little or no effect on the owners of ships. A good stout coat of paint would usually fool the underwriters, so ship and cargo were covered by insurance. As for sailors, there was an inexhaustible supply of them available from the Port Townsend crimps at thirty dollars a head.

The bark *Coloma* wasn't much more seaworthy than the *Southern Chief* when she towed out of Everett in December of 1906 with a cargo of fir lumber for San Diego. Built at Warren, Rhode Island in 1869, the old bark was long past her prime and, like the *Southern Chief,* she proved it by starting to fall apart shortly after she left the shelter of Juan de Fuca Strait and fell in with a southwest gale.

The *Coloma* had made scant seaway when the evening storm hit her, carrying away her mainmast, bowsprit and everything from the topmasts up on fore and mizzen. Throughout the long night the battered bark wallowed before the storm toward the dead lee shore of Vancouver Island, ships' graveyard of the North Pacific. The crew used bits of planking and deck cargo boards to fashion a raft, the boats having been smashed by sweeping seas and falling top-hamper. They hoped to launch the raft in the morning before the remains of the *Coloma* struck the rocks, but the raft was also swept away and with it went most of their hopes for ever reaching shore alive. They knew the Vancouver Island coast . . . a place of jagged rocks, impassable forests, angry surf, shipwrecks, death and desolation. And it was almost without human habitation. There was little chance of their plight being seen from shore, even if the *Coloma* lasted through the night.

At the keeper's house below the tower of Cape Beale Light, Tommy Paterson, his wife Minnie and

LOST AND FORLORN on the rocky coast of Monterey, the tiny 175-ton *Celia,* above, was one of the first of the steam lumber droughers, built by Turner at San Francisco in 1884. She stranded in 1906.

The *C. A. Smith,* below, was one of the largest of the wooden steam schooners, an 1800-tonner, built at the Kruze & Banks North Bend yard in 1921. She suffered a fatal stranding on the Coos Bay bar, pictured here, on December 16, 1923.

FORTY-EIGH
DOOMED!

SCHOONER WASHINGT
DRIVEN ASHORE!

GALE CATCHES HELPLESS VESSEL EMERGING FROM COLUMBIA RIVER

Schooner Smashed Down on Reef by Heavy Seas, Then Slowly but Surely Carried on to Destruction---Lifesavers and Tugs Unable to Reach Those Aboard Battered Hulk

THE WASHINGTON WAS DOOMED according to newspapers of November 13, 1911, for a smashing sea on the Columbia bar had loosened her deckload, smashed her hatches and jammed her propeller. She was drifting helplessly onto the ship's graveyard of Peacock Spit as night fell, and the lifeboats and bar tugs were held inside the river by the worsening storm.

The next morning, however, there was still water under the Washington's keel and the big bar tug *Tatoosh,* with Captain Buck Bailey at the helm, crossed the bar and worked her way into the breakers to get a line aboard the *Washington.* This nick-of-time rescue saved the steam schooner, her 25 passengers and 24 crew members, but most of her deckload of good Oregon spruce went overboard.

The *Washington,* 539 tons, was built at Seattle in 1906, is pictured above, left, as she appeared early in her career under Olson & Mahoney ownership. The dramatic rescue of the *Washington* by the *Tatoosh* is shown in the picture taken from the North Head lighthouse.

The *Washington* had many brushes with disaster and finally met her end in 1932 when she foundered in Humboldt Bay and her waterlogged hull was broken up for scrap.

their five children had remained wakeful until three o'clock in the morning while the building shook and the inshore gale tore the shingles from the roof over their heads. It was too wild a night for sleep and there was the likelihood of emergency calls on the telephone or telegraph as there had been eleven months before when the Pacific Coast Steamship Company's passenger steamer *Valencia* had struck on Walla Walla Reef and 117 of her people had died in the pounding surf.

Toward dawn keeper Paterson took a brief nap; then rose to put out the light. As he entered the glass-enclosed lantern room and looked out over the gray, white-capped sea far below he saw a disabled bark less than a mile off the grim cape, drifting straight for the rocks at its foot. The mainmast was gone, only a few shreds of canvas whipped from the rigging and the hull was so open to the sea that sections of the cargo were actually spilling out through great gaps in the rotten timbers. Seas were sweeping clear across her decks, but he could make out a man aloft waving a crude signal for help and others on the quarterdeck.

SHIPWRECK

Above, top to bottom: *San Pedro,* 456-ton wooden steam schooner collided with the iron passenger steamer *Columbia* off the Mendocino Coast on July 20, 1907. The *Columbia* sank in minutes; the *San Pedro* remained barely afloat, as pictured here, but survived until 1920, when she was sold to foreign owners. *Patterson* hit the beach at Yakatat, Alaska in 1938. *Alvarado* was a victim of wartime stranding on the Washington coast.

Right, top to bottom: *Hartwood* strayed too close to the rocks at Point Reyes on June 27, 1929, was subsequently smashed by breakers. *La Feliz,* stranded on the beach north of Santa Cruz on October 1, 1924. *Shna Yak* under tow through the Golden Gate after capsizing off San Francisco in 1916. *Klamath,* 1038-ton McCormick steam schooner struck the rocks off Del Mar Landing during a blinding rainstorm and 75-mile-an-hour gale on the night of February 4, 1921. All hands except the ship's cat were saved, but the *Klamath* was quickly pounded to pieces by the surf.

Paterson shouted to his wife and together they watched. It seemed hopeless, for once the wreck struck it meant almost certain death for her crew. Neither the keeper or his wife had any delusions on that score, but Mrs. Paterson was not one to give up without a struggle.

"The *Quadra!*" she exclaimed. The Dominion lighthouse steamer *Quadra* was lying at anchor in the shelter of Bamfield Creek. That was six miles away and the wires had been downed by the gale, as her call quickly proved. She turned from the dead telephone and pulled raincoat and sou'wester from a closet. She considered her rubber boots briefly, then discarded them for a pair of light moccasins.

Her husband knew what she had in mind. "I guess you'd better go, Minnie," he agreed. Maybe I can do something down on the rocks after she strikes, and you can't."

Half running, half staggering, the keeper's wife sped down the long, steep tramway, which was the sole human approach to the lighthouse. The storm and tide had converted the rocky peninsula inshore to an island. The water reached to her waist, but she didn't wait to launch a boat, but plunged in and waded fifty yards to the soggy but firm ground which marked the beginning of the Bamfield telegraph trail, a slashed track through the wilderness. Over or under fallen trees, ankle deep in mud and through the salt tide marsh of Mud Bay she ran, then out of the darkness of the forest where the surf roars and slithers clear up to the roots of the trees on Long Beach and back into the forest to the head of Bamfield Creek.

The area between the head of the creek and the seaward cove where the *Quadra* lay at anchor was supposed to be passable only by boat, but there was no boat. The lighthouse steamer was only two and a half miles away now and three miles and half beyond the *Quadra,* by the sea route, was the wreck of the *Coloma* with nine men aboard, drifting to destruction. Hardly pausing for breath, Mrs. Paterson gained the narrow strip of beach. Every hundred yards or so her way was blocked by jutting rocks or piled debris. If the water was shallow she plunged in and waded around the obstruction. If it was too deep she struggled up the bank and, crawling on her hands and knees, fought her way under the low-growing branches of fir and cedar and through the dense undergrowth of salal until she could reach the beach again.

BREAKERS AHEAD and a grim lee shore greeted the *Noyo* (2), ex-*Admiral Goodrich*, ex-*Aroline* on a foggy night in 1932 at Point Arena. This handsome little steel single-ender, operated by the National Steamship Company, went ashore and broke up near where the company's first *Noyo*, a 300-ton veteran of 1888 vintage was lost on February 26, 1918. A third *Noyo*, the former *Griffdu* (page 154) was placed on the Fort Bragg-San Diego run by National, but she was sold to new owners in Thailand after a year or two and the service was abandoned.

WRECK OF THE TRINIDAD provided awesome evidence of the might of a North Pacific storm, below. Outbound from Willapa Harbor with lumber for San Francisco, the 974-ton *Trinidad* ran head-on into a sixty-mile gale. Driven helplessly back toward the bar, the little ship struck on an outlying shoal off North Spit. The 36-foot motor lifeboat *3829* made the fifteen-mile run from Grays Harbor at the height of the storm and accomplished the almost impossible task of removing all but one of the *Trinidad's* crew. The second mate was swept overboard and drowned before the lifeboat arrived. The crew of the *3829* received the gold congressional medal for the outstanding rescue performance of that year.

ON THE BEACH AT PORT ORFORD, the W. R. Chamberlin steam schooner *Phyllis,* above, was soon demolished by pounding seas after straying ashore on the foggy night of March 9, 1936. The 215-foot *Phyllis* was built by the Aberdeen Shipbuilding Company in 1917.

Wartime wrecks, like that of the *Elna,* below, received little or no publicity.

A mile above the cable station, opposite which she knew the *Quadra* lay at anchor, was the home of Andy McKay, who was in charge of the telegraph line to Alberni. Only Mrs. McKay was at home, but she was the daughter of a former keeper of Cape Beale Light and it needed only the breathless words, "Bark coming shore", to enter her in the race to save the lives of the apparently doomed seamen. Together the two women bailed out a boat, launched it and rowed downstream toward the *Quadra*.

Captain Hackett of the lighthouse tender had just lowered a boat and was being rowed ashore when he saw the women approaching. It took them only a minute to gasp out their news. Ten minutes more and the *Quadra's* anchor was up, black smoke streaking from her stack and white water from her

LAST CARGO FROM GRAYS HARBOR to be carried by a wooden steam schooner was lost at sea when the Mexican *Salina Cruz,* the old Hanify Lumber Company double-ender *Anne Hanify,* caught fire and capsized off the Washington coast in 1949.

Calmar Line's intercoastal lumber carrier *Yorkmar,* inbound for Aberdeen, was blown off course while crossing the Grays Harbor bar in the winter of 1952, ended up high and dry on the beach just beyond the north jetty. Although given up for lost by most maritime authorities, she was refloated by the Astoria-based tug *Salvage Chief* in a remarkable salvage exploit, below; is still in service.

counter. An hour later she had lowered a boat, taken off the *Coloma's* weary crew and was steaming toward Victoria. The hull of the ancient bark was wide open, vomiting the holdful of lumber which, according to the shipowner's theory, should have kept her afloat.

Of course Mrs. Paterson didn't know that her race through the dawn and the storm had saved the crew of the *Coloma.* She was back on the forest trail fighting her way toward the Cape Beale Light.

The baby, she explained to the crew at the Bamfield Creek telegraph station, had to be fed—and she believed in feeding babies the good old fashioned way.

The theory of the buoyant cargo was tragically disproven in 1913 by the loss of the almost new

IMPALED ON THE COQUILLE RIVER JETTY, the lumber carrier *Oliver Olson,* wrecked there on November 2, 1953, was partially demolished by salvagers. The hull was then filled with rocks and is now part of an extended jetty which makes the river entrance safer for other ships.

steam schooner *Francis H. Leggett*. The *Leggett* was the latest word in coaster design, steel-hulled, full-powered with a big triple-expansion engine and double boilers, equipped with Marconi wireless. But an old-fashioned catastrophe befell her. Heavy seas started her rolling, the gripes holding down her deck-load of lumber broke and it shifted, giving her a list which exposed her vulnerable holds to the full fury of the ocean.

First reports of the *Leggett* sinking aroused rumors of a mysterious collision with the Japanese cruiser *Idzuma,* for the Port of Portland wireless station picked up the message from the warship, which thereafter lapsed into silence, refusing to give her location or any other details of the tragedy. This Oriental reticence delayed rescue efforts of other ships. Captain Mason of the coastwise steamer *Beaver* received the message from the *Idzuma* at 3:30 on the afternoon of September 18. It stated simply that the *Leggett* had sunk, giving no location. Captain Mason ordered his radio operator to contact the cruiser for further particulars, but there was no reply. It was almost midnight before the *Beaver* received a call from the Associated Oil tanker *Frank H. Buck,* reporting she was at the scene and had picked up one survivor. The *Beaver* changed course to join the *Buck* and from 12:30 until six o'clock in the morning circled the storm-tossed patch of floating lumber and debris which marked the big steam schooner's grave. The wooden steam schooner *Daisy Putnam* and the Standard Oil tanker *El Segundo* also joined the search, but only one other survivor was found, clinging to a piece of timber, and taken aboard the *Beaver*. More than seventy others of the *Leggett's* passengers and crew had gone down with the ship. James A. Farrell, one of the two survivors, was able to tell the true story of the sinking from a hospital bed in Portland:

"She was carrying a full load of lumber, about a million and a half feet, and a full list of passengers, between forty and fifty, along with a crew of twenty-five," he said. "Almost immediately after leaving Grays Harbor Monday morning we ran into heavy weather, which increased in violence until it was blowing a terrific gale. The steamer labored incessantly and could make almost no headway. Little alarm was felt, however, as the captain and crew told us the steamer would weather the gale. There was absolutely no panic, even when the final crash came."

Unfortunately for the victims of the *Francis H. Leggett* disaster, no compassionate eyes saw their plight from shore. The Imperial Japanese cruiser *Idzuma* might have saved many lives, but the warship's commander dispatched only the single cryptic message and ordered no change in course or speed. The other ships did their best, but there was only a slick of oil and a tangle of floating wreckage on the dark sea sixty miles south of the Columbia bar.

James Farrell, who was a young man of twenty when he escaped from the sinking steam schooner off the Oregon coast, is now an operating engineer living in Seattle and no one can convince him that a ship loaded with lumber won't sink.

The long shipwreck toll of years past is greatly lessened now; partly because of the new electronic aids to navigation, but more to the fact that far fewer ships now sail from West Coast ports with lumber cargos. Those that do each carry from five to ten times the cargo of the wooden lumber schooners, sail and steam, but even the big modern steel ships get into trouble sometimes.

In 1952 the Oliver J. Olson Company's 2000-ton coastal lumber carrier *Cynthia Olson* stranded at the north entrance to the Coquille River bar on the Oregon coast. That same year the Pope and Talbot freighter *Seafarer* grounded on the Columbia River bar and the Calmar Line intercoastal lumber carrier *Yorkmar* hit the beach just north of the Grays Harbor jetty. All three of these were salvaged, the *Yorkmar* in a particularly dramatic bit of work by the tug *Salvage Chief,* but the States Lines' Victory-type freighter *Pennsylvania,* beset by sixty-foot seas off the Vancouver Island coast, went to pieces as had the old barks *Southern Chief* and *Coloma* in those same waters decades earlier. It was presumed that the 46 men of the *Pennsylvania's* crew died in the boiling seas as they were launching the lifeboats, or did not get them over the side before the 7800-ton steamship plunged to the bottom.

The next year, in November of 1953, the *Cynthia Olson's* fleetmate, the 289-foot World War I-built *Oliver Olson* was headed for the Coquille River bar to pick up a lumber cargo at Bandon. Like the *Cynthia,* she ran afoul of strong cross-currents and heavy seas on the bar which swung her across the channel and into the rock jetty at the harbor's south entrance. There was no chance of salvaging the *Oliver Olson.* Three big holes were torn in her hull below the waterline, flooding two holds and the engine room, her rudder was jammed and her propeller fouled. She was there to stay.

Her stay became a truly permanent one when, after all her removable fittings including the nine-ton brass propeller were removed, the hull of the wrecked lumber carrier was filled with rock by the Army engineers. The *Oliver Olson* is now an integral part of an improved Coquille River jetty, helping to save other Bandon-bound lumber ships from the fate that overtook her.

In 1956, the year the Italian luxury liner, *Andrea Doria* collided with the *Stockholm* and went down off Nantucket, the Olson coaster *Howard Olson,* a 250-foot steel "stem-winder" staged a prelude to the Atlantic Coast tragedy. Off Point Sur on the morning of May 14, the *Howard Olson* collided with the 10,000-ton, 500-foot freighter *Marine Leopard.* The deepwater steamship sheared the little packaged lumber carrier completely in two.

The collision took place under mystifying circumstances with all witnesses agreeing that weather and visibility were excellent. The stern section of the *Olson* quickly went under after she broke in half. The freighter *John B. Waterman* picked up one survivor and one body, while the *Marine Leopard's* boats rescued the remainder of the steam schooners 29-man crew and two more bodies.

The scene of the accident, about thirty miles south of Monterey, is a busy shipping lane in the Pacific Coast trade. Both ships were equipped with radar and both crews agreed that the vessels were visible to lookouts for a full half hour before they came together. Many of the *Olson's* crew were fortunate to survive for the stern section, containing the crews' quarters, sank in three minutes and most of the men didn't even have time to don life jackets. Oil from the *Olson's* fuel tanks also complicated the rescue operation, as did the early morning darkness.

The bodies of the first and second engineers and the third mate of the lumber carrier were recovered. The steward apparently went down with the severed stern section and his body was not recovered.

The sea has never been tolerant of human error and the bones of other ships will, no doubt, find their resting place off the North Pacific coast to join the hundreds on the long roll of lost Pacific lumber ships.

Tongass

ROTTEN ROW

THE END . . .

OF THE LINE

Point San Pablo

. . . For the little ships of the coastwise lumber fleet.

Siskiyou

PICTURE INDEX

Special thanks is extended to William Hogan of the San Francisco *Chronicle* for numerous photographs reproduced in this book, and to the following authors whose works provided invaluable source material:
Ralph W. Andrews, *Redwood Empire*
Archie Binns, *The Roaring Land*
Edwin T. Coman and Helen M. Gibbs, *Time, Tide and Timber*
James A. Gibbs, Jr., *Shipwrecks of the Pacific Coast*
Jack McNairn and Jerry MacMullen, *Ships of the Redwood Coast*